Explorations in Language Study
General Editors
Peter Doughty   Geoffrey Thornton

LANGUAGE PROJECTS
An introduction to the study of language

Sandra Harris
and
Ken Morgan

EDWARD ARNOLD

© Sandra Harris and Ken Morgan 1979

First published 1979
by Edward Arnold (publishers) Ltd
41 Bedford Square, London WC1B 3DQ

British Library Cataloguing in Publication Data
Language projects. – (Explorations in
   language study; 12).
   1. English language – Usage
   I. Harris, Sandra II. Morgan, Ken III. Series
   428   PE1460
   ISBN 0–7131–0318–3

Explorations in Language Study

Language in the Junior School
E. Ashworth

Language and Community
E. A. Doughty and P. S. Doughty

Language Study, the Teacher and the Learner
P. S. Doughty and G. M. Thornton

Language, Brain and Interactive Processes
R. S. Gurney

Language, Learning and Remedial Teaching
R. S. Gurney

Explorations in the Functions of Language
M. A. K. Halliday

Learning How to Mean: Explorations in the Development of Language
M. A. K. Halliday

English as a Second and Foreign Language
B. Harrison

Language in Bilingual Communities
D. Sharp

They Don't Speak Our Language
(ed) Sinclair Rogers

Language, Experience and School
G. M. Thornton

Accent, Dialect and the School
Peter Trudgill

Printed in Great Britain by
Butler & Tanner Ltd, Frome and London

General Introduction

In the course of our efforts to develop a linguistic focus for work in English language, which was published as *Language in Use*, we came to realize the extent of the growing interest in what we would call a linguistic approach to language. Lecturers in Colleges and Departments of Education see the relevance of such an approach in the education of teachers. Many teachers in schools and in Colleges of Further Education recognize that 'Educational failure is primarily *linguistic* failure', and are turning to Linguistic Science for some kind of exploration and practical guidance. Many of those now exploring the problems of relationships, community or society, from a sociological or psychological point of view wish to make use of a linguistic approach to the language in so far as it is relevant to these problems.

We were conscious of the wide divergence between the aims of the linguist, primarily interested in describing language as a system for organizing 'meanings', and the needs of those who now wanted to gain access to the insights that resulted from that interest. In particular, we were aware of the wide gap that separated the literature of academic Linguistics from the majority of those who wished to find out what Linguistic Science might have to say about language and the use of language.

Out of this experience emerged our own view of that much-used term, 'Language Study', developed initially in the chapters of *Exploring Language*, and now given expression in this series. Language Study is not a subject, but a process, which is why the series is called *Explorations in Language Study*. Each exploration is focused upon a meeting point between the insights of Linguistic Science, often in conjunction with other social sciences, and the linguistic questions raised by the study of a particular aspect of individual behaviour or human society.

The volumes in the series have a particular relevance to the role of language in teaching and learning. The editors intend that they should make a basic contribution to the literature of Language Study, doing justice equally to the findings of the academic disciplines involved and the practical needs of those who now want to take a linguistic view of their own particular problems of language and the use of language.

Peter Doughty
Geoffrey Thornton

Contents

ACKNOWLEDGEMENT

We wish especially to thank all those students who have allowed us to quote from their language projects.

Introduction

'A substantial course on language in education (including reading) should be part of every primary and secondary school teacher's initial training, whatever the teacher's subject or the age of the children with whom he or she will be working.'

Recommendation 15 of the Bullock Report is making the basic point that no teacher should be innocent of the character and function of the medium by which he teaches and his pupils learn. Though elsewhere in the Report something is said of the possible content of such courses, nowhere is the critical question of approach discussed. Many students pass through such courses, however admirable in their design, yet remain innocent of the character and function of language, and unmodified in their attitudes to its uses in teaching and learning.

It is to this particular problem that our authors address themselves. They propose an approach to language study which takes as its basic axiom that, 'the study of language becomes more interesting for a student when he is allowed to take as his starting point some usage of language that he derives from his own experience. . . .' The student develops a Language Project in which he is required to '. . . describe certain features (of this usage) which he has discovered for himself'. In the process, students are drawn to '. . . make use of their own grasp of language in a way which we recommend they should do with their pupils', that is, they bring their intuitive understanding of language, derived from their basic competence as native speakers, to bear upon the usage they select as the basis of their Language Project and thus make explicit to themselves the rules by which the language itself functions. Thus the student is enabled to rehearse, in the course of the Project, precisely that approach which our authors recommend to him as a teacher when they suggest he must '. . . devise strategies to enable the learner to make explicit *what is already within himself*, the ability to use language effectively'.

This course does not begin with lectures *about* language, which can be processed by the student and safely tucked away as one more body of information, useful for passing examinations, irrelevant in the classroom. It begins by introducing the student to the idea of a Language Project. The student is then helped to choose a specific aspect of language use which he is to discuss and describe. When he attempts to do this, he discovers there is much that he needs to know, about language structure and language function, usage and attitude. The lecturer's role here is to act as consultant and provider of information sources. For the student, the Project is a self-educating process, whereby all that he finds out is active for him, because it is contextualized by the specific needs of the Project. As a result, positive changes of attitude are possible and the relevance of linguistic knowledge to language in teaching and learning made manifest.

Sandra Harris and Ken Morgan developed this approach at Nottingham College of Education, now part of Trent Polytechnic, and it is a particular merit of their book that one can see the process of development laid bare. They have had the courage to present their work, as it happened, without concealing the difficulties and disappointments such efforts must inevitably bring. Such frankness is a valuable guide to those who are encouraged by this account to attempt for themselves a Language Project approach.

While the book describes work done with education students, it must be said that the approach has a wide range of application. All those engaged with courses in Communication Studies, whether in school or college, or Language in the context of Social Studies and Sociology, would find much here they could exploit with profit in their own teaching situation. It will prove valuable, indeed, to those who are at the stage of designing new courses at the present time.

Peter Doughty
Geoffrey Thornton

1 The language study approach

Scene: George's Suburban garden.

Time: late spring.

Characters: George, an older man who has promised some bedding plants to an acquaintance from work.
Fred, a younger man who has high hopes of using what George will give him to make the garden of his new house less bleak.

George I've got them plants you want but I'll best show you how to put them in and keep them.

Fred Right oh, George.

George For bedding plants I've got you some Tagetes, Coccineum, Nicotianas and a few Oenothera Whitneyi.

Fred I thought *they* were called French Marigolds.

George Well, they are, but Tagetes is its proper name—same as Pyretheum is another name for Coccineum.

Fred Do you always name plants using the proper titles?

George When I can ... it keeps me in practice ... I've got you a few tomato plants and some potato sets but they're at the side of the lavatory.

Fred What's wrong with the proper name for them, then?

George (*smiling*) I can give them to you if you like ... Solarium tuberosum for the potato and Lycoparsicum erculentum for the tomatoes.

Fred Will these bedding plants stop in from year to year or will they eventually die?

George No, they'll snuff it at the back end of September, they're half hardy annuals, you see. The perennials I've got for you around the back with the veg. I've got a Cortaderia if you want one and a Passiflora.

Fred A what?

George Pampas grass and a Passion Flower. The Passion Flower will have to be grown up against a wall, though.

11

Fred	While I'm here, George, could you show me how to prune roses?
George	Well, you'll need some secateurs ... right back down the shoot ... leave two eyes and snip it off at an angle. Hold on to the end, though ... last year I was pruning a rambler and it shot back and hit me in the fizzog. How about a root of Mentha viridis before you go?
Fred	A root of what?
George	Mint. In the veg line I've got some Brassicas (*pointing to cabbage plants*).
Fred	Are they cabbage plants?
George	Yes. And some Phaseolus ... runner beans. I've got some lettuce. ... sod it, I can't think of its proper name ... and some Brassica olearacea ... Cauliflower ... but they're not ready yet. If you want any more you'll have to let me know. Don't forget ... are you harking? ... water them plenty if it's dry ... I was lucky, it syled down with rain when I bedded mine out.

The above text is the transcription of a tape recording of an actual conversation, made by a student on one of our language courses. At first reading it may seem no more than a slightly unusual dialogue, in that few gardeners are likely to use botanical terms in quite this way. But the more one discovers about the context of this situation, the more intriguing its language becomes. In the first place, George speaks with a very broad East Midlands accent. Having worked for many years as a labourer for the local council, he recently took up the job of porter at a nearby university. The student who taped this conversation describes the attitude of the academic staff to George's language as 'rather patronising and condescending; they think his pronunciation as quaint and something of a novelty'. George, however, refuses to change his language, despite pressure from his family to make adjustments, if only on such formal occasions as his daughter's wedding or for the sake of his job; and he fights off all attacks on his linguistic integrity with 'a mixture of resentment at change, cantankerous stubbornness and a curious pride'. The irony of the situation can be appreciated when we realize that the receiver of George's cabbages and wisdom is a lecturer on the academic staff of the university where George works.

Our point in introducing this, however, is not to raise issues relating to attitudes to language, but to use the extract as an illustration for two of our major premises:

1. That the study of language becomes more interesting for a student when he is allowed to take as his starting point some usage of language that he derives from his own experience and which he discovers for himself;
2. That because the student in this way is more conscious of the context underlying the text he chooses to study, he has a firmer base from which to relate the formal aspects of his text to the meaning, and better understands the complexity of the relationship between the two.

We feel that it is the neglect of this second aspect in particular which so often causes students to turn away from the study of language, seeing it more as a quasi-mathematical exercise in logic based upon invented texts, and for that reason both 'difficult' and 'divorced from reality'.

It may be that these arguments can be ignored with the captive audience of the secondary school where, particularly in the first five years, pupils have little option about what sort of language they will do. They are equally irrelevant for that small minority of students in Higher Education who for personal reasons decide to study Linguistics at University, whether as an independent discipline or in association with courses in Psychology, Sociology or Literature. But they are by no means irrelevant to those many students who expect, or are expected, to study language in some of the broader fields of Further or Higher Education. We refer to students taking courses in General Arts degrees, Teacher Training, 'Complementary' courses at all levels in Technical Colleges or Polytechnics, or 'General Studies' courses in the Sixth Form. Often the 'Language' of these courses is disguised under a broader title of Communication, or a less subtle designation like Formal English. Sometimes, when these courses form an integral part of a broader subject area like English or Education, they are justified with the argument that they ought to lead to a better understanding of the speech we use or the written texts we study, and are called, for the future teacher, Language and Learning, or Form and Meaning, for the General Arts undergraduate.

Whatever we call these courses, there are a very large number of students taking them; and most of us would probably agree that they all derive from and are related in some way to a vaguely defined area called Language. Our aim, however, is not to try and define what is meant by this area. Course content is not our concern, though we hope that the remaining chapters of this book will cover at least part of this ground. Our concern is rather with a method which can be used to introduce students to this area of study in such a way that they will not be provoked to the kind of response mentioned above. We have ourselves explored a method of doing this which we have found to be successful, and it is our experience in doing this that we offer in this book, together with examples of the work submitted to us.

To go back to the conversation at the beginning of the chapter, the student who used this as the basis of his Language Project found that, in being encouraged to collect his own text, he gained much more of a personal involvement in what he was doing and was thus encouraged to look for ways of meaningfully expressing the relation between the 'form' and the 'content' of the language. To put it another way, in needing to describe certain features which he had discovered for himself, he was less reluctant to shy away from, even ready to try and invent, 'technical terms', which he now found necessary merely to state what he wanted to say. It is essentially the difference between needing *noun* or *sentence* to express precisely a certain relationship and being told what Nouns and Sentences *are*. We stress, however, that we are not trying to offer a course in Language. We are merely trying to set up an awareness in our students that a course in Language need not be irrelevant to their needs or too difficult for them to do. The 'course' comes after the 'project', and leads, one hopes, to other, better disciplined and more precise projects.

The Language Project: general aims and organization

Some years ago we were faced with the task of teaching a slot in the timetable called Language. Our first approach to this was to fill the weekly session by trying to teach the students some appropriate terms and then use these terms—ranging from *register* to *delicacy*, *clause* to *pronoun*—to back up our discussion of appropriate texts. This largely derived from our own experience as students. It was the way we had been taught and we found little reason to question it, particularly since much of the teaching we found going on around us at the time was conducted in the same way in most areas of the curriculum. One question we never asked ourselves was whether we had not objected because we personally rather enjoyed working in this way, and in any case were interested in this kind of language study. We soon found, however, that many of our own students did not enjoy this process of defini-

14

tion and analysis, at least where language was the object of examination. We soon began to wonder why, after careful preparation, on our part, most of the students were simply not interested in the fascinating intricacies of *phrase structure* or *nominal groups*; and the necessity of a small number of staff having to do this with a large number of students, with the resultant need for having a lecture programme, added considerably to our disenchantment.

Ironically, it was these very difficulties which proved to us how imperative it was to rethink our whole teaching philosophy, at least where language study was involved. We were finding it impossible to 'teach' anything worthwhile, considering the time available, the scope of the overall programme and the number of students. Since at that time our students were trainee teachers, we also were conscious of not following one of our basic precepts—that in some sense they should make use of that fundamental grasp of language which their own future pupils would have as speakers of English, even before they ever arrived in the schools, and make this the lynchpin of their teaching method. We were clearly not doing as we preached. With an abrupt change in direction, therefore, we stopped 'teaching' our students and decided we would try to get them to 'learn' something from within their own experience.

To change a teaching method in such a radical way on the basis that the one being used does not seem to work is not always justifiable, as the teacher rather than the method may be at fault. Obviously we need to look much further than at the discomfort of lecturers and students. There were, undoubtedly, a number of ways in which we could have changed our approach. Most of what follows is an account of the method we chose as being suitable to our own institution, with its particular curriculum, staffing and timetabling problems, and to the kind of student we found in our classes. We shall expand on this in the next section. What follows is a brief account of the method we began to employ and of the kind of situation to which we feel it is adaptable.

Our approach has been to allow each student to carry out an investigation which we call a Language Project. At the simplest level this means no more than letting students find their own language texts for study and then use their own experience, helped by that of their tutor, to comment on that text. Because the texts are their own 'discovery', and they are already familiar with the situation in which they obtained them, they will have sufficient start to make pertinent remarks, if only at first about the content. We argue, in principle, that when students examine texts in this way, they quickly come to the point of asking questions which are common to all texts, but from what is to them a more meaningful, because more personal, base. When they have, for example, asked 'Who said that to whom?' of a particular text it is not difficult to generalize the *who* and to *whom* to any text and arrive at the categories of *producer* and *audience*. The point is that, in producing these categories for themselves, the students find them more accessible and realize more immediately the need for them than if they were just informed about them. In other words, we try to let the students produce their own descriptive categories, encouraged by a tutor who is prepared to offer help by asking simple questions about the knowledge the students already have.

The crucial first step in this method, then, is that the student starts essentially from an area of his or her own choice. When students have made a choice of text to be studied, as we describe in Chapter 6, we meet them individually or in groups of two or three to discuss their work. These tutorials are principally devoted to an exploration of problems and terms appropriate to the task. We do not pretend that the outcome is always happy, since many students find the task of thinking objectively about their intuitions rather difficult. We did not find it easy ourselves, nor were we able to devote the time we would have liked to each student. But even so, two things have been most reassuring.

The first is the extent to which students respond to being given their own heads and to using a 'knowledge' of language which they never realized they had; once, that is, they get over the initial trauma of not having formal constraints and 'given' information—a process they find rather bewildering at first.

The second encouraging fact to emerge from our experience is how many students can be dealt with in this way. At first sight it seems virtually impossible for one teacher to see fifty or more students tutorially in one year when this aspect of his work barely covers a quarter of his load, as has been our case. That it can be done at all stems from our first point, that one is not teaching in the formal sense, but utilizing existing knowledge.

We stress, however, that we look upon this method as no more than an introduction to the study of language. A student who has been put into this position of self-examination is more likely to feel the need for a structured course at a later date, since one of the outcomes of doing such a project is not only to make the student aware that he is able to say more about language and language usage than he previously thought possible, but also to

16

motivate him into realizing how useful the terms associated with an established model are in talking and writing about language. Our experience is that a student who has written a Language Project in the first year at college is likely to come to a second or third year course, where close examination of a text is required, with a much better awareness of the relevance of linguistic theory and description to his needs as a user of language in any context. He also comes to such a course with more confidence that he is able to do it.

Although many of our students have been involved in Teacher Training, it is principally in the main subject area of English that the work we quote from has been done. We also use it as a component of English as part of a Humanities degree, where it performs the same role of being the introduction for all students to the study of language, and as part of general social and cultural studies on various technologically-based degrees. Time and opportunity have not enabled us to experiment far with it in the area of professional training for intending teachers, but what little we have done in this direction has proved to be an excellent way of getting students to bring language under a personal and immediate scrutiny. The only difference here from the general approach is that the text for examination is in some sense an educational one, varying from a transcript of language interaction in the classroom to evaluation of a series of passages showing a child's development in writing to a review of the language of a textbook. If a student tapes his own classroom technique, it can also be of great help on teaching practice.

Finally, we believe that an approach to the study of language based on this kind of introduction can be adapted to local differences for many situations in Colleges of Further and Higher Education, especially in those areas not dominated by examinations. We agree that, for it to work, some flexibility will be required both in attitudes to timetabling and perhaps also in the notion that sometimes prevails in many such institutions, that the only worthwhile educational activity is where teachers face their students in situations of information passing. We have been lucky, no doubt, in having met with this kind of flexibility in our own institution; we see no reason why it should not occur elsewhere.

The College Setting

As the remainder of this book is an account of our own experiences with language projects in a Polytechnic, perhaps a more detailed description of our particular situation would be helpful. Most of the students we are concerned with are in their first year. They all take English as one of a total of three subjects. These will vary from student to student, but will include History, Geography, Biology, Art, French, and Education, according to individual choice and whether they are following B.A. or B.Ed. courses.

Nearly all these students have passed O-level English Language and A-level English Literature, and might therefore seem to be well prepared for the kind of work they are being asked to do in their language project. Of this we remain unconvinced, since the study they are now being asked to carry out is different in kind from any of the work they have previously done. This may of course change as more students become familiar with studying language along the lines of *Language in Use*; but few of these have yet worked their way through to Further and Higher Education.

If our students have any advantage at all, it is probably in their experience in focusing upon texts in their A-level work. One might suppose that this makes them in some sense intuitively 'aware' of subtleties and nuances in stretches of written language. But this is often outweighed by the disadvantages which their previous approach brings with it. For example, many students tend to view 'language' as predominantly literary. Their main interest lies in examining their own response, and they find it difficult to look at language in any other way. They often have strongly entrenched attitudes towards 'correctness'. For them the 'language' of a text exists only in its alliteration and imagery, and there is often great difficulty in getting them to tackle non-literary texts. Perhaps the greatest problem we meet as teachers is that our students are so accustomed to being 'told the answers' that for the first few weeks of their work with us we are forced to spend considerable time simply trying to convince them that they can actually ask their own questions. It would be foolish to pretend that we always succeed.

It is interesting that some of the students with whom we have the least difficulty in this question of attitudes are those who take a science as their second subject. For example, such students do not think twice about using such a term as *category*. They usually see a positive advantage in doing so. On the other hand, some students brought up in more purist schools of literary studies find it difficult to come to grips with the notion that to attempt objectivity need not damage their response to literature.

One other item can be mentioned here, and that is the extent to which our students are familiar with grammatical terminology. All have met such common notions as *sentence* or *verb*, though usually with the connotations 'making complete sense' or 'a doing word'. Some are familiar with *clause* or *phrase*, to the extent that a few schools still seem to put their pupils through the mill of clause analysis. Apart, however, from those few who look upon the idea of using such terms with complete horror, even sometimes as 'educationally destructive', most students are prepared to come to some understanding of them. What we can say is that the knowledge of these terms that they bring with them tends to be misleading, or else they bring very little of it at all. Consequently, we operate on the principle that we develop an appropriate terminology as we go along, and on the whole this works reasonably well.

If the kind of students we have dealt with over the years has remained more or less constant, our approach to language study has changed considerably. We emphasize that the procedures described in detail in Chapter 6, **Problems and Procedures,** have been gradually evolved over a fairly long period of time.They are intended to represent a working model, not a fixed set of directions. We fully realize that the classroom calls for flexibility and compromise; and we are ourselves subject to the pressures of time, numbers, examinations and competing subjects which most teachers too often experience.

Hence we have decided to present our 'results', in the form of student language projects, before our 'method'. The studies put forward in the succeeding chapters have been selected not because they are the best or the most sophisticated we have received but in order to demonstrate what can usefully and feasibly be done by ordinary students with a little direction, and to discuss some of the problems involved in the process. We hope not to evoke the response that 'My students aren't up to that', but rather 'My students can do better than that!' Though quotations, of necessity, must be limited, we would like to give some ideas as to:

1. The methods of collection, e.g. accessibility, equipment, difficulties involved.
2. The actual source material.
3. The analysis of source materials by the student.

19

We must add here only a few further comments on the language areas selected. Obviously, the breaking down of language into distinct areas has to be in some sense arbitrary. There are always many possible divisions, depending largely on one's point of departure and intended focus. Moreover, a certain division usually presupposes others and imposes its own limitations. For example, one could divide language into only two areas, written and spoken. But even such a broad division would limit the student whose focus is a written–spoken contrast or who wants to use both written and spoken texts, while focusing on some other aspect such as idiolect or the language of the seminar.

Thus the areas which we present in this book have a practical rather than a theoretical orientation, in that large numbers of students have found them useful in the selection of their individual projects. They are not meant to operate as a theoretical framework in any sense but merely to suggest certain starting points, a practical guide to the feasible. Some of these areas are deliberately overlapping so as to impose as few initial limitations as possible, while at the same time providing vague guidelines which can be made more specific and given direction and focus as the project progresses. There are numerous other areas which could have as easily been chosen. As it was obviously impractical to present samples from, or even to describe all possible aspects of, language study, we have included a fairly lengthy list of some of the projects which we have supervised in the *Appendix* in order to provide further suggestions.

As a final word in this chapter we add the following caution. There is always the danger of underestimating a student's potential in language study from what often appears a naively developed language project. It is all too easy to hurry along a student's fumbling towards expressing his ideas about language by giving him a suitable ready-made model. Whether this description will derive from Generative, Systemic or Traditional grammar is beside the point. The method we are advocating demands that the student himself should be encouraged to see the need for such a model and for a precise and adequate description. Hence we have elected to work towards an appropriate terminology as the need arises. It is for this reason that we often accept, in our students' projects, attempts at descriptive adequacy which, by the criteria of an approach more firmly based on Linguistics, might seem no better than gaucherie. But we firmly believe that a student comes to a better understanding of his problems by trying to tackle them in his own way, and the realization that there are questions to be asked can often be more rewarding to a student than to be told the answers to questions posed by his tutors. Moreover, as we said before, the kind of student with whom we are dealing is not likely to come into our courses with a predetermined desire to study Linguistics, and there is consequently the danger of over-estimating the effect of one's own enthusiasm. It is easy, with these students, mistakenly to assume that because we, as teachers, may find Linguistics interesting, our students will equally be fascinated by it. Rightly or wrongly, Linguistics has acquired the reputation of being a difficult subject. No student was ever convinced to the contrary merely by being told that this was not so; and our experience has been that putting the General Arts student through a formal course in language description, let alone Linguistic theory, converted very few of them to this belief. It is mainly for these reasons that we have emphasized context as much as, if not more than, formal categorization in developing a student's work. This can give the impression of too little attention being paid to structure and to much to meaning. But this is, after all, what the student is most familiar with; and that is where we wish to begin.

2 Casual conversation

As we have emphasized earlier, dividing language into areas of manageable dimensions is, at least partly, an arbitrary process. One such division, which we have found to be a useful one that allows for a variety of possible approaches, is what we have labelled 'casual conversation', perhaps the most readily accessible of all language areas. All of us each day experience a continuum of such language, whether it be over the breakfast table, in the market, at coffee time, or waiting for a bus. These conversations form the very bedrock of social reality for the ordinary person. As Ogden and Richards put it, 'throughout the western world it is agreed that people must meet frequently, and that it is not only agreeable to talk, but that it is a matter of common courtesy to say something even when there is hardly anything to say.[1]

This kind of language is sometimes called 'phatic communion', defined by Malinowski as 'speech in which ties of union are created by a mere exchange of words' and 'language used in free, aimless, social intercourse'. In either its public or private form, phatic communion has provided a convenient starting place for a number of our students, and what follows are excerpts from the texts and commentaries of the language projects of three students who have selected this general area as a focal point. Two of the sample studies deal with phatic communion directly, one in a very limited and totally intuitive way, the second involving some background reading and a general widening of scope. The third student selects for her text a conversation between two elderly sisters and investigates the differences in their respective idiolects (the language of an individual) as well as their social interaction. All concentrate on spoken language, though the third project also includes two letters which might well be described as written forms of phatic communion.

22

The first student describes the initial stimulus for her project in the following way.

The stimulus for this assignment came when I accidentally recorded my mother holding a lengthy conversation with someone attempting to sell a central heating system to her. The woman concerned appeared to be merely after 'leads', which her employer would follow up later. The actual 'sell' of the system was not successful but I obtained a fairly accurate tape of the situation.

On playing it back I was somewhat surprised to find that I had not really listened closely to the actual language but only the general meaning of the conversation. For example, the woman trying to sell the central heating had a marked nervousness, which appeared on the tape in the form of lengthy pauses while she thought of another argument, aimed at defeating my mother's indifference to the product.

The pauses became more and more obvious as the tape continued until the woman was forced to conclude the conversation and, somewhat apologetically, leave. I was interested to find that my mother had not realised what exactly she was saying, nor the effect she was having on the woman ... I did not transcribe this particular piece of tape but decided that if I were to choose several examples of this, or something similar, then I would probably discover much more about the language used than by merely listening to a tape which would probably be forgotten quite soon after listening.

This student then goes on to describe the subsequent taping of her mother's interaction with three regular callers: a breadman, an insurance man and a football coupon agent. Having placed a cassette tape recorder beside the door, she simply requested that her mother switch it on each time a caller arrived, and the recordings obtained were of sufficient quality to transcribe. With regard to the three callers selected for study, she states,

They were chosen, partly for their individuality from all the other callers and partly because each has a different relationship with my mother. This made me realise just how important the person who answered the door would be, for it depended to a great extent upon the reaction which my mother exhibited and exactly what her knowledge was of these men.

Roughly: Subject No. 1—had a positive effect upon my mother, in that she responded quickly to his 'newness' at the job.

Subject No. 2—I was aware of an antagonism between them from the beginning.

Subject No. 3—appears to be quite a friend of the family in an indirect way and is treated as such, with reservations, of course, as he is still a salesman of a kind.

Although the student did encounter some difficulties with the tapes (such as outside noise), here is by and large an exceptionally feasible type of project. The situation was kept constant; there was a common participant; very limited stretches of language were involved; the emphasis was on social interaction. The full text comprised five interviews with each subject, at intervals of a week. We have extracted the first and second interviews with each caller.

Subject No. 1—First Interview   Breadman, age 28

(*Dog barks*)

Mother   Bess, be quiet! (*closing door, agitated*)

Breadman   Mornin' love, 63 pence, please.

Mother   Oh, you're the new man on today, are not you?

Usual man   (*Shout from across road from the usual man.*) Here, Col, somebody else talking about you again?

Breadman   Yes. Great to be famous, in'it?

Mother   I reckon it's getting pretty bad, the weather, heaven knows when spring'll be here, eh?

Breadman   Well, it's certainly cold enough but better than that blizzard we had yesterday.

Mother   Yes (*laughing*).

Breadman   Well, thanks ... er ... very much, love, see you tomorrow. Ta ra.

Mother   Righto, ta ra.

Second Interview

Mother   Oh, hello, you're a bit early today, are not you?

Breadman   Yeah, s'pose I am really. I wanted to get back early, before two today, to see about the car. It's been playin' up again.

Mother   Oh heck, we've been getting trouble with ours

	for the past two months. My husband reckons it might be something to do with the back axle (*laughs*). I don't know that much about cars y'see. Just leave it to the men.
Breadman	I dunno, it's not worth leaving it to this man. I've had cars for about six years now and still don't know anything about 'em.
Mother	Sorry, I have not got any other change.
Breadman	Oh, it's okay. Always like this on a Friday—pay day, thank God!
Mother	Don't I know it. See you on Monday. Thanks.
Breadman	See ya. Ta ra (*whistles off down the path*).

Subject No. 2—First Interview   Insurance Man, age 25

Insurance man	Hello there! (*briskly*)
Mother	Hello (*not really enthusiastic*). (*Papers exchanged.*) You're a little bit late on the rounds today, are not you?
Insurance man	Oh—erm ... yes, really.
Mother	Car hold you up then?
Insurance man	No, not really, not that. (*pause.*) Well, thank you, bye-bye.
Mother	Ta ra (*closes door*). Never said a blinking word, that bloke. Had his pen in his mouth all the time, he did.

Second Interview

Mother	Hello. (*handing over books.*)
Insurance man	Hello. (*Silently fills in books.*) Well, thanks very much. I'll be back next week, same day, I reckon. Bye.
Mother	Ta ra then (*door shuts heavily*).

Subject No. 3—First Interview
Football Coupon Collector, age 55

Mother	Hello. Coupon, right again, eh?
Collector	Yep, that's it, Mrs. Thomas. They say time stands still for nobody, don't they? How's your mum, then? It must be all of twelve months since I was on the round.
Mother	She's doing fine really. Decided to move from Sefton Avenue. Our Ivan's buying her house

25

	and she's having Ray's while he buys another one in Peel House Lane.
Collector	That's great. Did you say Ray's the youngest of your four?
Mother	Yes, he's the baby of the family, I s'pose.
Collector	I don't know, I could never keep track with all the kids who used to be on that round in Farnworth. What with you and Craigs next door, all looked the same to me.
Mother	I'm sure my mum got us all sorted out (*laughs*).
Collector	Well, I should hope so. Well, I've gone on for long enough. I'll see you next week.
Mother	Righto. See you. Ta ra.

Second Interview

Mother	Hello.
Collector	'iya. I'm in a really good mood tonight, I can tell you.
Mother	That's nice to know anyway—but you always seem to be like that, Mr. Burton.
Collector	True, true. Not many days I feel down in the dumps. Have to keep the customers happy anyway. You wouldn't want an old sour puss knocking at the door, would you?
Mother	No, no (*laughing*). Keep at it! Well, here's the Littlewoods coupon. I can't think what's happened to the Vernon's one. Ken must've forgotten to fill it in, or else he left it at work. Never mind, I think there's an agent at work who'll take it off him.
Collector	Well, as long as we don't miss out on a fortune, it's all right. I'll see you then, Mrs. Thomas. Ta ra.
Mother	Ta ra. See you.

Despite (or perhaps partly because of) their extreme 'ordinariness', these transcripts are quite intriguing. Here we have the material of everyday 'talk' which most of us engage in only semiconsciously, but which provides an excellent text for the exploration and analysis of language in context. What does the first year student, with little guidance from tutors and none from books, make of it? Here is a sample passage dealing with 'the establishment of the relationship':

This must always occur at the beginning of a relationship and consists of the usual greeting characteristic of each subject. In the case of Subject 1, my mother is establishing a truly new relationship and not just one which has lapsed in the period of a week. For this reason then, the establishment of a relationship, or communication, is extended to the centre or climax of the meeting. It does in fact form the core of the whole of the first meeting. After this point, the greeting is kept basically the same, allowing the core of the situation to be different.

The greeting changes only twice, once when in the second interview my mother is surprised to find him there so early and in the fourth when she forgets to bring out her money.

In the case of Subject 2, the greeting is kept extremely formal and varies very little. This repetition is even extended to the point where any form of greeting used by one person is exactly reproduced by the other. This could show antagonism or indifference, certainly little enthusiasm. The greeting in this case is characteristically as sparse as the other two sections.

Subject 3, because of his unique relationship with my mother, varies his greeting format a great deal. He immediately establishes a very informal relationship by using the name 'Mrs. Thomas', while my mother in turn uses his name quite naturally. Greeting here then is much more informal and less important in the actual buying and selling process.

I presumed then that the establishment of a relationship plays an important factor in determining the form which the core of the meeting will take. As in Subject 2, poor establishment means inadequate central discussion and general collapse of relationship which proves to be final in that no communication is ever shown to be made.

This is the work of a student with little formal experience of language study, either previously in school or in college, and the intuitive quality of the analysis is evident in her struggle towards concepts like 'phatic communion' and 'formality', lacking as she does the terminology which would help her. This becomes very evident when she tries to deal with sentence length.

The most important thing which I discovered in studying this was that lengthy sentences did not necessarily denote an intelligent person. Subject 2 was of a higher intelligence than either 1 or 3, yet his sentences were inhibited and thus kept at a minimum of an average of about five words, while the latter two extended their sentences far beyond this.

The lengthier two subjects also composed their conversations of small paragraphs, whereas no. 2 failed to do so, due to lack of subject matter about which to talk. He tended to restrict his words to monosyllabic answers or phrases like 'See you next week', or 'Thanks very much', nothing which could have meant anything specific or personal.

Another interesting factor which I noted was the continual use of questions while conversing between each other. Subject 1 was especially obvious on this point and so was my mother, which suggests that it was a combination of the two which led to this situation. Its function I could not determine, unless by way of nervous reaction by two people who do not know one another.

In this passage the problems of the student become fully manifest. It is interesting to note, first of all, her association of 'intelligence' with 'lengthy sentences', which though it may seem very naive for a student in College, suggests a misconception about the nature of language which is very widespread. One wonders also how she came to the conclusion that 'Subject 2 was of higher intelligence than either 1 or 3', and the implication here is of another widespread misconception which associates intelligence with social class and status. The lack of adequate terminology forces the student into an extreme awkwardness of expression, which the use of such terms as 'text', 'utterance', 'exchange', 'interaction' would have done much to alleviate. The student's use of 'paragraphs' for describing a stretch of spoken English, for example, highlights this need for more precise terminology, and probably also indicates the predominant emphasis in most schools of the written forms of language. Though this student has an A level in English, this is the first *spoken* text she has ever attempted to analyse, which goes some way towards explaining her difficulties.

On the positive side, however obscurely she expresses it, the student senses the way in which the 'context of situation' influences what is said rather than speech taking on predetermined and fixed patterns. If this seems rather obvious, it is surprising how often students do not find it so. This student notes the presence of questions, but is unable to take this further, either in terms of formal analysis or function. She concludes with the following paragraph:

The whole assignment then has made me much more aware of the language which we speak and of our bland use of words

28

which mean so much, yet are rolled from the mouth to be forgotten almost immediately they are said. I honestly enjoyed this piece of research and could have continued in other branches had time permitted, finding enjoyment not only in the implications of the language but in the way in which we assume our roles in different situations, with different people.

As we hope these sample passages indicate (the project is much longer in its entirety, but these quotations are fairly representative), this piece of work represents a first attempt by a below average student to look closely at social interaction of a very limited kind, a stretch of 'real' language, and to extract its underlying 'meaning potential', to borrow Halliday's term.[2] Although unsophisticated and imprecise in many ways, this kind of project does involve an inductive approach to learning through the raw material of language; it does provide a genuine experience of the study of language and a basis from which to develop more sophisticated and meaningful concepts.

Compare this student's rather limited approach with that of the next student, who has also chosen to focus on phatic communion. After an introductory discussion of Malinowsky's concept, he selects five different settings involving different participants: 1. His own home when a cousin is introducing his fiancée to the student's parents. 2. A book shop in which the owners greet a visiting salesman. 3. A casual meeting in a railway station between the student and a stranger. 4. An interview between a tutor and a prospective student. 5. His mother and father over tea.

Here is the railway station conversation:

Situation D
i. Location: A railway station.
ii. Those involved: An unknown man and myself.
iii. Relationships: No previous encounter had been made with the man. It was necessary for me to be directly involved in this situation as I wanted to observe a strictly one-to-one relationship. I assumed the role of a reserved person in order to test the theory that it is necessary to break silences. It was impractical to use a tape recorder in this situation as there were obvious dangers involved if discovered taping the conversation. The stranger's reactions are more important than my own, as these are undoubtedly the most natural.

29

iv. The conversation:

(A very long silence to begin with which I was determined not to break—though significantly I found it very difficult to remain silent.)
Man   The train is late, isn't it?
Myself   Yes, it is.
Man   Have you been waiting long?
Myself   Long enough. It's probably a holdup somewhere.
Man   Yes probably. Still there's no hurry.
Myself   Are you going far?
Man   Not very.
(At this point, the man began to look round the room. I decided to ignore what had effectively been a verbal signal not to question further.)
Myself   Business or pleasure?
Man   A little of both.
(The man's tone of voice and obvious annoyance at my continuing questions suggested that it would have been unwise to remain any longer. I therefore left.)

The construction of this situation is fairly typical of all such meetings between strangers. The first statement merely invites the agreement of the other person. The man is in no doubt as to whether the train is late or not. He knows that there is not likely to be any great disagreement on what is after all an indisputable fact. Similarly he is not interested whether I have been waiting long or not, it is merely a small piece of common experience that he knows us both to have had. This securing of agreement in the first few minutes of an exchange, on insignificant matters, is an important function of phatic communion. Having agreed on two things, the lateness of the train, and the length of time that I have been waiting, I then gave him the opportunity to agree with something that I said. Consequently there is now some indication that this stranger is willing to hold a conversation. However, my question as to how far he was going was one that provoked a defensive response. The man obviously did not want to tell me where he was going. In a normal situation this would have been sufficient indication not to proceed further with the questions on this particular subject. However, I decided to press the man, and therefore ignored his verbal signal. His annoyance at this was a direct result of my deliberately ignoring the signal. Phatic communion should have prevented the embarrassing situation that was to follow. Phatic communion is here establishing the possible areas of further conversation. The man obviously was not willing to discuss his private business, and he tried to hint this in his non-commital response. Had I taken notice of his signal and moved the exploration to another field (e.g. the weather), the possibility of further exchanges would still have been there. As it was the man was now

30

unwilling to talk anymore at all. Phatic communion is used in this situation to avoid such scenes arising.

Here again we have a readily accessible situation which can provide illuminating material for language study. Although the student's analysis involves nothing technical, his background reading material and his understanding of phatic communion and verbal signals are obviously an advantage. His level of perception also appears to be higher than the first student's, perhaps in part because of his greater precision in expressing himself. In the case of both students, the collection of language source material which they are required to examine as closely as possible significantly sharpens their awareness of language situations and makes them conscious of language operating in social relationships in a specific context and for specific purposes, which are not always immediately evident. Phatic communion, approached either way, makes a convenient starting point because it is so common and accessible, because it seldom involves more than short stretches of speech, because its surface features are usually obvious enough for even the least able student to identify some of them and, not least, because it is so often entertaining. Indeed, this student's transcript of his parents over tea reads like a real life version of a Pinter play:

Situation E
So far all the exchanges that I have reported have had one thing in common, they have all been between relative strangers, where there has been an element of tension in the situation. However, phatic communion does not only take place between strangers. It also occurs between good friends, and even husband and wife. Therefore it can be assumed that phatic communion serves some other purpose than breaking silences and creating a speech situation.
i. Location: The home of my parents.
ii. Those involved: Mother, father.
iii. Relationships: Self-explanatory. The conversation was recorded using a concealed tape recorder.
iv. The conversation:
(Father has just returned after a day at work. Mother is a housewife.)
Wife   Hello, love. Had a good day at the office?
Husband Not bad, and you?
Wife   The coalman came. Here's your tea.

Husband	(*sits down at table*). We had a new man start today from the other works—Bill something or other—quite a nice bloke. Did you go shopping.
Wife	No, the coalman was coming. I told you.
Husband	Oh yes. The tea's very nice. What's for pudding?
Wife	Apple pie. It's been cold again.
Husband	Did you hear from your mother?
Wife	No. Do you want the sauce?
Husband	It's about time we had some warmer weather. Yes, please.

I have not indicated the pauses that occurred in the exchange. These pauses occurred quite frequently, and the exchange is more a series of unrelated phrases, rather than a continuous exchange. The conversation is almost a ritual, and something very similar must be seen in many houses in the same situation. The exchange does not convey any great information from one partner to the other. It is significant that the two principal pieces of information that are uttered are either forgotten (in the case of the coalman's visit), or is not referred to by the other partner, (the new man at work). The exchange arises more from habit than a real need to communicate. The words are empty ones and on their own are insignificant in themselves. They do, however, fulfil a useful purpose in keeping what might be called the lines of communication open.

No matter how well people know each other they still like to talk together, even when there is nothing to talk about. There is a need to keep open passages of communication once they have been opened up, and phatic communion fulfills both functions. If good friends did not speak to each other then they would obviously think that something was wrong ... because doubt can exist in the silence. Therefore the exchange between the husband and wife described above can be seen to be checking that the communication lines are still clear between both partners. If some new situation had developed during the day that the husband was unaware of, and that had caused some kind of unspoken (at this point of time) rift to have occurred, then the new situation would become immediately apparent during this period of phatic communion.

This then is the essence of phatic communion, which can be either public or private. As the student suggests, phatic communion is a ritualized exchange which serves a purely social function and avoids embarrassment at the public level or the sense that something is wrong at the private level which silence nearly always implies. The 'message' in terms of the passing of information is nil, or almost nil, and the exchange itself becomes the vehicle of certain feelings or attitudes. Of course one could argue that the passing of information is in any case only one of a number of functions of language, and what the student calls 'the lines of communication' refers to a much wider concept including the affective and social functions of language as well as the ideational, which is concerned with the actual content of what is being said.[3] The emphasis here must be on the interaction, on the sense in which the situation, the participants and their roles *create* the language used and limit the possibilities and the range of expression in a marked way. These projects represent only two of a number of possibilities which, as a sub-area, phatic communion makes possible for language study.

The third student has selected a focus which is probably outside phatic communion but still falls within the general area of casual conversation. After a lengthy description which includes family background, education, occupations, social class, and relevant past experience of two elderly relatives, she recorded the following conversation. The sisters are discussing the idea of returning goods to shops; Nan is presently employed in an electrical shop.

Nin   He could come back to you and change those tubes.
Nan   I said he could change it.
Nin   Yeah. Yeah.
Nan   But not the money back.
Nin   Oh yes, that's wrong. Yes, you can have your money back anywhere now. You can have your money back. The man was talking on the television, the man, about everything and he said—you heard it, Cynthia—and he said, 'Don't get misled with these shopkeepers.' He said, 'If you want your money back,' he said, 'you can demand it back, demand your money back.' And there was no hesitation at—er, where did we go and get our money back? No hesitation. They can't, they can't refuse it now, no, they can't.
Nan   Well, no names, no facts—you all know this person, this lady, and you'd swear, your life by her and only that she'd slipped up and she'd—we caught her. Only she bought a bulb from me and—er—she took it. Anyhow in about two hours she brought it back. She said, 'I'm sorry, Mrs. Calow, as soon as I put it in the light, it popped right away.' 'Oh,' I said, 'well, we always exchange, not a refund.' And I said, 'We always—er—exchange what you buy, but just

33

	a minute,' I said, 'this is not our—er—packet.' 'They're both yours,' she said, so I looked at the bulb and it wasn't our make at all.
Nin	Ah, well, I mean, that's different, isn't it. You couldn't expect to go to another shop and change something you've had from somebody else's shop.
Nan	I know, I know.
Nin	But, I mean, what you get at any shop—I mean, I mean, I wouldn't go to a shop and take it back if it wasn't—
Nan	And I was thinking after—you know what she's done, don't you. She's brought the one back that had gone originally, that's what she's done and kept the one at home that she's said she's from us, and that's the fact of it.
Nin	He said, 'It's these shopkeepers, don't like it now because they can't do anything about it now. They've got to refund your money,' and he said, 'Remember, always remember,' he said, 'You can refer back to the—er—' What is it? The weights and measures, is it?
Nan	No, no.
Nin	No, not weights and measures, but it's something (*pause*). There's no shop that can't not refund your money back now (*pause*). Look at my boots—went back with that firm, no hesitation, give me the extra money back. No, oh no, same with the manager, give me the money back. No hesitation.
Nan	I'm not arguing about that.
Nin	Eh?
Nan	I say, I'm not arguing with you because that's not right.
Nin	But you can't, you can't, can you, when I've proved it, can you.
Nan	No, but, you see, you're talking about shoes, but I'm in electrical.
Nin	But it doesn't matter, it's the same but different. Anything you buy you can if you're not satisfied with it, if it's not to your satisfaction, you can have your replacement or your money back.

Besides being amusing, this text provides some interesting language material, which might be explored in several ways. First of all, it is a good example of 'real' spoken language, especially as it was produced spontaneously and was taped without the knowledge of the participants. We have found it interesting to compare, with a class, a transcript such as this one with a similar stretch of dialogue taken from a novel or a play, when it becomes

34

immediately apparent just how controlled and ordered art is even when it attempts to simulate disorder and casualness. Here are some of the student's observations:

The most striking difference in this part of the tape is the use by each sister of complete sentences. Nan, in her tale about the lady returning the light bulb, mainly uses complete sentences, giving her speech a storylike quality and a sense of logical progression. Unperturbed by interjections by Nin she completes what she wants to say and her story has a marked beginning, middle and end.

Nin, on the other hand, rarely uses complete sentences in conversation or indeed in written language. She talks as she thinks, the same as most of us do, but has a great deal of difficulty in expressing herself coherently. She also had difficulty in recalling previous events so that her arguments are confused and hardly ever reach a definite conclusion. She frequently asks questions, but, never waiting for an answer, she carries on regardless to the best of her ability. She repeats herself profusely when she can't think ahead enough to continue the sense of her speech.

Although these remarks are at least partially based on the text, one rather suspects here that the student's prior knowledge of her subjects, and her preconceptions of their language, are strongly influencing what she observes. Though it is generally true that Nan's story is more coherent in the sense of 'a beginning, middle and end' than Nin's, *both* participants demonstrate in a marked way the characteristics of spoken language and are not nearly as easily distinguishable as the student suggests. (Obviously, we are thinking of the transcript here rather than the actual tape recording, on which the two speakers *sound* quite different.) Her comments, while they have a certain validity, are much too general; and the numerous use of pauses, fillers, false starts, repetitions, sentence fragments and interruptions by both participants are largely ignored, perhaps again in part because the student lacks terminology.

One might note also her pre-occupation with the 'complete sentence', which she does not define or relate to specific examples from the transcript. As with the first student, she is probably thinking in terms of written language, which is far removed from this particular example of speech. It is also interesting to note that the student attributes Nin's lack of coherence to 'talking as she thinks', while describing Nan's utterances as having a 'storylike quality', both of which also indicate certain ideas about the nature of language which need to be further explored. What is most lacking in this study, however, is the close textual analysis that both of the first two students, however inaccurately, attempted and which is essential if the student is to come to terms with his material.

Apart from spoken language, the text also provides a good example of social interaction.

It is important to remember that this conversation is between a potential customer and a shop assistant and each is therefore biased towards her own situation.... The conversation ends in stalemate as each refuses to give way to the other. This is true of many conversations and arguments which we all have. Each person is biased to begin with and, despite attempts to sway the other, both remain stubborn in their own insistence of their own knowledge. Each sister has, in fact, only half of the story, but neither really listens to what the other has to say. 'I'm not arguing with you', says Nan as she has not seen the television programme to which Nin refers. 'But you can't, you can't, can you, when I've proved it to you, can you,' says Nin in reply, but has she proved anything at all? She knows what she wants to say but finds immense difficulty in communicating her ideas verbally in a logical form which people can understand.

As the student comments, we have in this text a striking illustration of, on one level, a total lack of communication. Nin misses the point of Nan's story about her customer completely, and their responses to one another become increasingly unrelated until Nan is forced to declare in desperation, 'No, but you see you're talking about shoes but I'm in electrical.' This conversation seems to us all too typical of the failure of participants who start from differing points of view even to listen to each other. In this rea too the comments of the student need to be more detailed and explicit.

As we mentioned earlier, this project also includes several samples of written language, namely, personal letters. Here is Nin's:

16 Claremont Drive
Wi hockey

My Dear Angela,

Well Dear I am glad you are all right and meet some nice Girls @ you are happy I miss you very much, But I don't mind so long as you are happy and have a nice time. and look after yourself. I am glad the food is all right @ you like, Well Dear all the Dogs is all right they all send their love to you I will be seeing you soon. I going to post it

All my Love to you

Love aunty Francis nin

x - - - x good night
Darling

This might be described as a written form of phatic communion. In what other possible context could dogs all send their love? The student in her commentary recognizes the link with speech but fails to explore the meaning of the letter as it relates to levels of formality.

When looking first at Nin's letter the correlation between her spoken and written language is obvious. She writes in the same style in which she speaks. If you define a sentence as ending with a full stop, then there are only two sentences in the whole letter. The letter is made up of numerous clauses joined by conjunctions such as 'but' and 'and'. Unhindered by full stops the letter does flow, as there are no divisions for paragraphs. Her knowledge of the correct form of letter writing is limited to the basics, such as the address on the top righthand corner and opening on the left. There is however no comma after the first line and her use of capital letters is somewhat inconsistent as words such as 'dear', 'dogs' and 'but' all appear with capital letters throughout. She leaves unfinished sentences.

Instead, she falls back, as students so often do, on the idea of 'correctness' in a very limited sense, largely in terms of capital letters, full stops and commas. Certainly it is not very helpful to identify sentences in this context solely on the basis of full stops nor is it true that 'she leaves unfinished sentences'. There is only one unfinished sentence in the letter, and this is clearly the kind of oversight found frequently in casual writing. In her eagerness to justify her statement that 'she writes in the same style in which she speaks', the student fails to read what is in the text. The issue is obviously more complicated than this; though Nin's letter may be more like casual conversation than most business letters or an advertising circular, there are still some important differences which reading the letter aloud establishes quite clearly. One would not mistake this letter for ordinary speech even without the letter format. The student goes on to criticise the writer for her 'lack of logic', which again seems somehow beside the point. Viewed as phatic communion, the letter is quite effective. Its message is simply that 'I miss you and care about you, and don't worry about things at home.'

These studies then are a few of the possibilities which the area of casual conversation yields. We emphasize that though these examples are in one sense completed projects, in another and more important one they are merely a beginning, a prelude to further study and understanding. It is our experience that students can only take in so much by way of introductory concepts and terminology and that the 'learning through doing' approach now so prevalent in the primary school is also applicable in the context of studying language. This is particularly true in the area of 'correctness', where attitudes towards language are likely to be firmly entrenched. Seminars and lectures can be devoted to the subject in which students nod sagely or even agree enthusiastically to suggestions that 'correctness' is not absolute but related to levels of formality, social acceptability and function; yet, we have learned that these discussions make little real impression unless the student is actively engaged in exploring for himself some aspect of 'real language', and these same students are as likely as not to revert to their original attitudes soon after leaving the seminar room. If there is any doubt about the nature and strength of such attitudes, one has only to note the reaction to Peter Trudgill's book *Accent, Dialect and the School*, in which he suggests that no dialect or accent (including standard English) is inherently superior to any other. He received literally hundreds of 'attacking' letters

38

from the general readership when the book was published, many of them, one suspects, from English teachers. So perhaps it is only to be expected that many of our students share these attitudes. Consequently, as we have said previously, the sample projects presented in this chapter, and indeed in all the succeeding ones, contain inadequacies and problems which we have made no attempt to conceal; rather, we have made use of them as possible points of departure. On the other hand, we hope they are also interesting and illuminating, both in terms of the material collected and analysed and as a basic structure which can be extended in many directions to suit the student's language needs and interests.

3 Dialect, register and idiolect

These three areas of language study are perhaps best discussed together, because any student who chooses one of them almost invariably becomes involved in the other two. Besides being popular choices with students, they can be sources of considerable confusion. This confusion is perhaps compounded by linguists, who do not agree among themselves on a definition of dialect, and whether there is such a thing as register, much less how to recognize its various forms. Difficulties also arise from the inevitable overlap and interrelatedness of these areas of language study. The boundaries between them are far from sharp and clear. Though a full discussion is impossible here, and in any case there are already many such published,[1] it may be useful to offer some guidance of a fairly elementary nature.

Idiolect, perhaps the simplest of the three to define, can be regarded as the language of an individual. It is primarily speech but can also include writing. Usually what you can *hear* from someone is more distinctive than the writing you can see. Any analysis of idiolect must take into account phonology (not only individual features of pronunciation but stress, intonation, rate of speech, pitch, voice quality, prolixity, etc.), vocabulary (including also idioms and use of cliché and metaphor) and grammar (with particular emphasis on features deriving from dialect and social class).

Obviously, there are idiosyncratic elements in each of these areas, and the resultant whole is unique to each individual. However, both dialect and register figure as very important aspects of a person's idiolect. The student wishing to study idiolect must be aware of as many environmental and social factors (including past ones) as possible in relation to his subject, as well as the context in which his recording or interviews take place. He must be prepared to try to separate the idiosyncratic linguistic features from those of a particular dialect. He may be concerned with a single tape, in which case shifts in register are probably minimal, or he may be interested in obtaining deliberate contrasts in register through a series of tapes in differing contexts.

Dialect presents more problems, but probably for the purposes of language projects it is best to simplify and accept the idea of an approximate 'standard English' (though without clearly marked boundaries) with dialects as the non-standard (not *sub-*standard) forms spoken in particular regions. In terms of analysis, dialects involve varying features of grammar, vocabulary and phonology. In this connection two further problems might be mentioned.

1. The choice of a participant. Does a given participant speak standard English with a regional accent, or does he speak a dialect? The matter of accent comes in here. As it is usually very difficult for students to manage an adequate phonological analysis, we suggest, if possible, that students select a speaker who exemplifies other features as well and genuinely speaks a dialect.

2. Dialects are also closely related to social class, and many linguists regard class dialects as separate from regional ones. This too is something to be taken into account. Again, it is often difficult to separate a class dialect from a regional one, as there are many overlapping features, but students should be aware of the possible distinctions.

Register is perhaps the most difficult term to deal with, and the difference between register and dialect is not in any case absolute. Dialect may indeed function as a register, as in the case of a London businessman returning to his home region for a stay with his elderly parents who live in a remote farming village, or the student who speaks standard English in his seminars but Geordie with his flatmates who also come from Newcastle.[2] Alternatively, registers have aided the development of certain dialects. One student writes the following of the Liverpool dialect and its origins:

One of the most obvious groups of words to study is that with naval origins. The Liverpool dialect naturally has a great many of these. Some are extremely obscure or in little use so only those in general use with fairly well-defined sources have been chosen.

'Go hard astern' is colloquially used as advice to give up. The phrase can be seen to derive from the naval order to turn around and is used similarly in civilian life. 'Scuppered' has been adapted also from the merchant navy term to mean finished or defeated. The phrase, 'hung, drawn, and scuppered,' has long been used in the dialect to imply that a person deserves punishment.

'Sling the hook' is a term widely used on Merseyside to express annoyance or dissatisfaction. Originally dockers would cry, 'Sling the hook' before finishing work, the hook being their unloading tool. During the early part of this century when there was much dissension over docker's wages, the cry was heard frequently during strikes and has since become incorporated into the dialect.

One can trace elements of the influence of register in this sense in most dialects.

Though there are several different definitions of register, it seems to us that there are two aspects to consider when approaching register with students. If we regard register as language in a particular context, language in use, then we can emphasize either the *use* or the *user*. If we focus on the *use*, then we can look at the register of different occupations (e.g. law, physics, trawlermen, doctors) or particular contexts (mothers talking to children, telephone conversations, cocktail parties) and the multiplicity of subdivisions possible and necessary to make these manageable. This need not be a superficial approach and may well involve more than one speaker (or written text). It could involve focusing further on grammar (or an aspect of grammar, lexis, phonology or particular phonological feature). The degree of technicality, level of formality, medium, and subject matter provide additional dimensions.

If we choose to focus on the *user*, then we are more concerned with differences, with register switching, and the total situation which prompts the user to alter his language in significant ways and match the particular linguistic features to the overall contextual meaning, with all its subtleties. Students find this an extremely difficult but fascinating area of study. In this sense, all of us have not only a variety of different registers but intuitive feelings as to how register operates which can be explored and made conscious and explicit. One must add that the two aspects of register mentioned are not mutually exclusive but a matter of approach and emphasis, and indeed students should be encouraged to consider both when collecting and analysing their texts.

42

If this discussion seems to raise more questions than it answers, the sections which follow contain more explicit and detailed discussions and examples from various student projects which deal with these areas.

Dialect

When they are asked to think about a topic for a language project, the first idea which occurs to most students is dialect. This is by far the most popular *initial* choice, and for a number of reasons. First of all, it seems easily accessible and obvious, being one of the few areas of language study with which students are already familiar and which they think they know about. Secondly, the prospect of looking at a dialect is likely to capture the interest of the student immediately, and it is nearly always the dialect of his home region that he suggests studying. Here is something for which he has a special affinity, which is likely to be heightened by his being away at college. And, thirdly, there are more secondary source materials available on dialect than on many other areas of language study; many newspapers print columns (such as 'Jabez') celebrating the local dialect, and, with a little searching on the part of the student, books or parts of books or articles can usually be unearthed which contain helpful information in the form of language history or word lists.

At this point we must issue a word of warning. Dialect has proved in our experience one of the trickiest and least successful areas of language project work, and the forementioned reasons for its appeal to students actually seem to militate against the completion of a satisfactory project. First of all, because the student does feel he already knows about dialect, he is less likely to consider the problems involved in the study of it. His approach is more likely to be haphazard and his methodology ill-considered, and he feels less need for tutorial guidance than he otherwise might. Dialect is the one area in which students apparently suffer from over-confidence. Secondly, the fact that he is studying his own dialect actually gets in the way of his analysis. It is always much easier to analyse other people's language, particularly when deviations from a norm are involved, than one's own. The problems of identifying vocabulary items and grammatical patterning are compounded, and the whole area of phonology tends to sink into a morass of inaccuracy. Moreover, if he is at college, the student is likely to be some distance from his home area and hence has

43

to fit all his research into holidays, which makes the possibility of a rushed and superficial study a special consideration. Lastly, secondary sources often prove a hindrance rather than a help. Newspaper columns are often contrived and exaggerated; books are usually out-of-date, and in any case encourage the student in the direction of pure hack work. Copying out long lists of vocabulary items from a book is of very little use to anyone and produces work which student and tutor probably find equally tedious. Unless the student is prepared to discuss and meet these problems, dialect as an area for study is probably better avoided.

Still, having emphasized the dangers of dialect, so to speak, we offer some suggestions for those students who are yet undaunted by the known hazards. Of first importance is the production of a text, which must take the form of a tape recording or perhaps several recordings, which must then be transcribed as accurately as possible. This text may be supplemented by other source materials and observations and interviews, but a central text is absolutely necessary to ensure genuine research and originality on the part of the student. Also necessary, and it is surprising how frequently students need telling this, is a complete description of the participants and the total situation which elicited the text or texts. This is one student's account of her attempts to get a text of a particular dialect, Mow Cop in Staffordshire.

Initially, I interviewed only my grandfather, but I came to the conclusion that this did not represent a true cross-section of the community, and consequently attempted to enlarge my language source. In the main, the group consisted of older inhabitants, ranging from about fifty-five years of age to about seventy-three years of age. It was in this age range that I expected to find a greater source of the unique Mow Cop language. However, I did include people of younger ages, including my father of forty-two years, and of course I depended somewhat on my own language, the unique nature of which was brought to my immediate attention when I left home for college and mixed with people from all parts of the country.

I discovered that all of the men I interviewed had completed their national service at one time or other during their lifetimes, and that nearly all of these men had returned to Mow Cop soon after. About half of the men were in fact born in Mow Cop, and this included both my father and grandfather. One of the men was in fact born of a Mow Cop father, and this was in itself extremely valuable in my study of the village language.

44

Each of the men did have, of course, very different backgrounds and equally different occupations, ranging from demolition workers to potters. Several of the women in my group also worked in the potteries for a considerable time of their lives, but few were actually born in Mow Cop. Two were born on nearby farms and quite a number did actually come from the five towns themselves. One extremely lively seventy-five year old was actually born in Mow Cop, but travelled to Lincoln at the age of fourteen to become a chamber maid at a large house there. However, this lady was invaluable to me in her stories of childhood, particularly concerning childhood games of her time.

Of the men and women who were not born in Mow Cop, almost all of them have lived there for at least twenty years, which did seem to suggest that they would speak the basic Mow Cop language, although, of course, many other influences, both geographical and occupational are evident in their speech. And, of course, many of my interviewees were much more responsive than were others, so presenting me with greater material for my text. However, I feel that I can say that all of the people I talked to contributed to my research greatly.

I began to collect my text at the earliest stage possible, but was of course somewhat restricted by being approximately fifty miles away from my main language sources. However, I began to record all of the words that I could recall from Mow Cop, also asking the girls in my block at College to write down all the words I repeatedly used in normal conversation. Now I had begun to collect the beginnings of my actual language text.

In the main part, then, the text was gathered by listening to the villagers themselves, attempting to record at every snatched moment. During the conversations I attempted to guide my interviewees into certain lines, but also to allow them to speak as freely as possible whilst trying to say as little as possible myself. Again I tried to do as little writing as possible during the actual interviews, fearing that I might create a strained, unnatural atmosphere so limiting my chances of a successful study.

This makes interesting reading and illustrates some of the problems involved in dialect study and how one student attempted to solve them, though this student obviously does not go far enough in describing the context and the participants. Occupation, age, social class, past experiences, family, personality all play crucial parts in the language we speak and must be documented as clearly as possible, not hinted at. Furthermore, the language situation itself (Was the participant nervous? Put off by the tape recorder? Speaking differently from his usual manner? How well does he know the interviewer?) must not be left vague and general if the analysis is to have any real validity.

In addition, it is better to have a clear idea of the focus of the project before the collection of the text, though in practice this does not always work out as planned. The number of participants is important and in part will determine what the student can do with his text. Probably the easiest approach is a single text from a single participant, in which case idiolect must be considered in conjunction with dialect. Here is a part of the text of a student looking at English as it is spoken in Brunei. Her subject is a student from Brunei, who is studying in England.

I can't really categorise what sort of educations I've received. I just remember that I went to a Malay school and then to an English school. In Malay school I studied for about four years where we were taught the basic knowledge of Maths, language, drawings and then as we go higher we studied a bit of geography and history and we did lots of physical educations as well. But when I went to an English school after four years being in the Malay school, the same thing happened again as we were prepared to go into this more or less the secondary equivalent of the English schools. This is for three years from Prep One to Prep Three. We studied the same basic things except of course that the medium in which we studied this was in English. The difficulty being was that having no knowledge of the second language in which we were taught then, I found it's very difficult to understand the teachers. Most of the teachers who were teaching me they came from England, Philippines, Malaysia and India and because of this, I think the varieties of accents that has been expressed to us is a bit confusing.

The student goes on to analyse Bruneian English, using this one tape as her starting point. This is perfectly acceptable, and this particular tape contains a great deal of material, as the deviations, especially in grammar and phonology, are quite marked. The student, who is also from Brunei, in many ways finds the analysis more difficult than would a native English speaker, though she is also helped by her knowledge of Malay as, for example, when she looks at her subject's handling of tenses—

The Malay language does not have any tenses. The verb used is the same regardless of its present, future, past and continuous

46

tense. Whether an action is to be performed, was, or going to take place, it is merely indicated by an addition of suffix and prefix. In our attempt to write and speak in English, we are continually confronted by difficulties in grammar, idiom and their usage generally and we find that these difficulties arise most frequently from those words which do not obey the rule derived from the majority, like the words forming irregular past tenses and participles. This can be seen in the recorded example with regard to the verb 'choose'.

The English of foreigners, though not strictly within the definition of dialect, provides a fruitful source of study for some students. Superficially the deviations from standard English are easy to spot, though further categorizations of errors, particularly in the area of phonology, often proves very difficult, as indeed it did in this case.

On the other hand, the student may aim at eliciting a contrast. He may interview dialect speakers of different generations, and indeed this is both feasible and interesting. He may tape speakers belonging to different social classes, occupations or even sexes. Whatever he selects, he is likely to be more successful if he works out his intended focus in advance.

Assuming then that the student has collected a text or texts of his chosen dialect, the analysis often presents further problems worth mentioning. Initially we said that a dialect as we see it involves differences from 'standard English' on three linguistic levels: phonology, grammar, and vocabulary. Certainly it is extremely difficult for students to tackle all of these with equal fervour, though not impossible. Phonology seems to present by far the greatest number of difficulties for students but cannot be avoided altogether, as even a transcript requires some attempt to come to terms with 'sound', whether the student adopts the International Phonetic Alphabet or some system of his own devising. This is further complicated by the need to suggest intonation, pitch, pausing and stress.

Generally speaking, we do not recommend that students attempt to describe dialect (or any other form of language) in terms of the International Phonetic Alphabet, which is very cumbersome to use, hard to read, and is more than likely to be used inaccurately. Except for the rare student who is really fascinated by phonology, the I.P.A. produces a description more delicate than most student language projects require. Students who choose to focus on phonology should be recommended to read Abercrombie's *Elements of General Phonetics and Linguistics* or O'Connor's *Phonetics* (Penguin), which will familiarize him with linguistic terminology and, more importantly, make him aware of the complexities and subtleties of any system for describing the sounds of language.

We most often suggest that either students adopt the descriptive key found at the front of most dictionaries or else that they devise some system of their own. For example,

Cockney Pronunciation

w Pure except for the slight distortion of the following vowel: wol—why woat—what plus impact of the glottal stop on 'without'—wi-vaht

v Contaminated by f—'verh' becomes 'fvrey' (often followed by 'likely' or 'i', a very important phrase which, according to the tone in which it is spoken, can indicate any feeling from boredom to excitement)

n Substitution for m for n, n for m:
I went to see the Pamtomine.
I saw a lot of enty bo' 'les near a lanpost.
We have Enbassies all over the Enpire.
It was very enbarrassin', it was.
We were in this tent made of camvas.
I was imformed that I was in Emfield.
The cellar was imfested with near se'em 'undred rats.

There are some inaccuracies in this account but on the whole, for the student who is only incidentally interested in phonology, this, or something similar, seems a happier alternative. If the student is dealing with intonation, stress, pausing and pitch as well, then the picture becomes all the more complex. Crystal and Davy have devised a system in *Investigating English Style* which the more sophisticated student might find useful; for others, and this probably includes the majority, again we recommend the student to devise his own markings and apply them to his text.

Describing the grammar of a dialect adequately is only slightly less difficult for most beginning students than describing its phonology. Probably the greatest obstacle is the student's lack of an adequate terminology, and his failure to utilize his own intuitive knowledge. There is no real answer to this except a number of tutorials during which the tutor and the student can go over the

48

text together and devise categories which the latter is capable of handling. Grammar is usually the area in which students feel most inadequate, and, not surprisingly, their knowledge is often greater than they realize. In any case, we have usually found it better to build on the student's own knowledge, however meagre, and the linguistic terminology with which he is familiar, usually that of traditional grammar, rather than launching him into a transformational or systemic description or some other theory which serves only to confuse him *at this stage.*

Brunei English
There is also a confusion over the use of singular and plural because he is not quite used to the idea of the rule governing the use of singular and plural. When the speaker says 'we did lots of Physical Educations' he is led to assume that whatever follows after 'lots' will be in the plural. This also applies when he considers 'educations' as a massive subject and that it has to be in the plural as the case may be if he speaks in Malay. Therefore, the difficulty is realised not so much over 'countable objects' as it is in 'noncountable objects', and even more when a collection of something is involved.

Lincolnshire dialect
As a result of my investigations a number of interesting facts emerged. For example, in the verb 'to come' an unusual pattern appears to have developed. To illustrate this pattern I will use the four basic forms:

present tense—I come
past tense—I comed
past perfect tense—I have comed
future tense—I will come

Notice in this irregular verb the second and third forms remain almost the same, contrary to the pattern of standard English. Such a pattern suggests that confusion has arisen as to which is the correct form, for there has been an obvious attempt to make the irregular verb 'to come' into a regular verb, since the endings of the second and third forms are identical to those used in the regular verb 'to walk' in Standard Modern English. The unusual pattern which has developed in the verb 'to come' again recurs in the verb 'to tell', for example

present tense—I tell
past tense—I telled
past perfect tense—I have telled
future tense—I will tell

but in standard English it is in the second and third forms: 'I told', 'I have told'; although they remain almost the same, they do not add 'ed' to the verb in the present to make the past tense. This tendency to standardise verbs by adding 'ed' may also be observed in the verb 'to see'—'I see, I seed, I have seed,' also in the verb 'to know'—'I know, I knowed, I have knowed.'

This pattern is not merely characteristic of Newton and surrounding villages but is peculiar to the whole of the county. The examples above are just a few of the irregular verbs that have suffered as a result.

In making this study of verb patterns I also discovered that a degree of confusion occurs, by many people in Newton, when using the verb 'to be' in the past tense. When speaking in the plural instead of saying 'they were' or 'we were', they persist in using the singular when referring to more than one person, for example: 'we was', 'they was'. This is a fairly common grammatical error in Newton. However, I am uncertain as to whether this mistake is yet again another characteristic of the Lincolnshire dialect or in fact universally made by people throughout the British Isles regardless of where they live.

These two excerpts represent the kinds of grammatical descriptions one can expect from first-year students with no previous experience of language study. They are of course not the whole, but extracts from respective sections on grammar. The first shows the student moving in the direction of 'count nouns', and she gets her point across fairly well. The second example, dealing with tense and analogy, is less satisfactory in terms of concision and clarity, but this student too is able to make her comparison. At this stage one would not expect a more sophisticated description of the intricacies of tense in English, greatly oversimplified here. There is, however, a decidedly pejorative tone to this study, which illustrates how difficult it is for students to look at dialects objectively and not in terms of 'mistakes' and 'errors'.

The second example brings up a further problem, that of distinguishing a social class dialect from a purely regional one. Indeed, the student indicates her uncertainty, and the grammatical forms she mentions in this extract are more closely associated with social class than with a particular part of Lincolnshire. As mentioned earlier, this distinction is a difficult one to make, but provides in any case useful material for discussion purposes.

Vocabulary is probably the most obvious and seemingly easiest aspect of a dialect to study, and here we encounter the dangers of the word list.

Mow Cop dialect
Personal behaviour—words
kerch—injure
jed—dead
kempt, klempt—starving
slat—throw
poopeyed—surprised
chatting—scratching your head
jim jamming—gossipping
laubed up—filthy
mincing—strutting in high heels
tick over—have 40 winks, snooze
ommer—hammer
shindigging—dancing
firk out, wriggle out—take something out
face—cheek, insolence
sheed—spill, drop
nesh—feel the cold easily

Personal behaviour—phrases
make ructions up, make a palaver—make a commotion
she's knick-knocked—she's mad
she's over the top—she's mad
she's losing her buttons—she's mad
I'll give her a good tanking—I'll give her a good spanking
go neck over crop—go head over heels
write keggy-handed—write with your left hand
wool gathering—day dreaming
be cheeky hard faced—be cheeky, insolent
don't use your face to me—don't be rude, insolent, to me
tip the mink—pass information, let in on the secret

These words and phrases are indeed based on an original text and the list (which is considerably longer) is the result of the student's own research and observations. They would be much more helpful if they were related more closely to that text and placed in a context instead of paraphrased. Also, classifying them in terms of areas such as 'personal behaviour' serves no real purpose, and the student needs to discriminate a little further. For example, 'ommer' for 'hammer' seems to be based solely on phonology rather than lexis; 'to make a palaver' has as much grammatical as lexical

51

interest; and words like 'mincing' and 'wool gathering' are not really dialect words at all but in general use. Although interesting to note, a list such as this one should be used as supplementary material to a text.

Here is another example, looking at Cockney rhyming slang, where the student has used secondary source material to augment personal observation:

Bird lime: 'Time' (1857). 'Time' here refers to a sentence served in prison. It is again metaphorical—once you're in it, you can't get out of it.

Bottle of spruce: Twopence (1859). This is rhyming slang on 'deuce' or two. Obsolete.

Brass tacks: Facts. I had, for some reason, always believed this to be a Yorkshire expression, but H-G has it as Cockney rhyming slang; it is an interesting example of how many rhyming slang phrases have become generally colloquial.

Bread and butter: Gutter (late 19th/20th century).

Bread and cheese: Sneeze (recent).

Bread and jam: A tram (20th century). Originating about the time of the 1914–18 war and becoming obsolete with the trams.

Bristol City: Titty. Another of the most well-known—and used— phrases in rhyming slang and another that has travelled beyond its Cockney origins. 'Bristol' is another of those phrases that cause the mind to boggle when one attempts to see through to its original meaning. I can only imagine the young ladies of Bristol to be particularly well-endowed!

Bubble and squeak: To speak (mid 19th/20th century). Also, the Beak (Magistrate); thus, to Bubble—to carry tales to the authorities.

Bull and cow: A row (1859). The marvellous imagery employed here obviously implies some sort of marital upheaval.

Bully beef: Chief.

Bushel and peck: Neck. Cockney comments on the nature of married life!

Cherry hogs: Dogs (recent). I presume that this expression refers to the greyhounds who run on the dogtracks rather than the average domestic hound.

It is both interesting and useful for the student to use the Old English Dictionary and other references in tracing the history of particular dialect items, but in our view this should not be the focus of a language project. Many students also like to include a history of the dialect in general terms, and this too can be illuminating, but only as the background to an original text.

Another possibility is to examine dialect through the use of questionnaires, and a number of our students have done this. Though questionaires are most often used in connection with dialects to determine the currency of certain lexical items (one student looking at Cockney rhyming slang examined the language of different generations in this way), they can also be focused on language attitudes, with some interesting results. Obviously, good questionnaires are not easy to devise or to analyse, and if this one lacks somewhat in sophistication, it does reveal some interesting and, from the point of view of the linguist, rather disturbing attitudes towards language:

Questionnaire and Results on Cockney Accent

Question 1. Are you ashamed of your accent?
Most people (75%) admitted to being ashamed of their accent.

Question 2. If so, why?
Do you think that the London accent is legitimate as regards the history of accents?
Has it a history?
Do you believe the accent to be largely attributable to laziness?
Do you think *your* accent betrays your social class?
People who admitted that they were ashamed of their accent quite often believed it to be related to their social class (about 57%)— i.e. that most Cockney speakers gave the impression of being working class. Relating this to Question 4 I asked them if they thought that the same applied to a Yorkshire accent. Just over half said 'no' but one or two people remarked that it might be so within Yorkshire but that an ignorant outsider could not differentiate between different levels of accent. Many thought (78%) that the accent was lazy. Some even thought that it was entirely due to this and had no legitimate antecedents (23%).

Question 3. If not, how would you describe (i) your accent and (ii) your attitude to your accent?
Some of the 4 people left who were not ashamed of their accent said that they had no particular attitude to their mode of speech— in which case it is interesting to look at their reaction to Question 4. One person said he was actually proud of his accent.

Question 4. What would your attitude to your accent be if you came from say, Yorkshire, Cornwall, Wales or Northumberland?
Or if you came from Liverpool or Birmingham?
Would you try to modify your speech to something which more closely approximated to Standard English?

About 80% said that they would make no attempt to modify their accent if they came from say, Yorkshire, but also about 75% said that they would if they came from, say, Liverpool. Thus it seems to be partly a question of what seems to be considered 'attractive' and thus acceptable.

Question 5. Do you try to modify your accent?
If so, under what circumstances?

Almost everyone admitted to having tried to 'put on' an accent, and the fact that the figure was higher than the 75% of Question 1 indicates that some people are suffering from some sort of misconception in their answer to Questions 1 and 3. After all if they felt the need to modify their accent they must feel to some extent that it is not acceptable. Those who spoke with marked accents said that they tried to speak 'better' when they felt unsure of themselves or inferior: with business colleagues, teachers, or tutors. A small percentage, including some of those who were not ashamed of their accents in Questions 1 and 3, could be considered people with Standard English accents. They said that at times they changed their accent to become more Cockney because they felt out of place in a circle of people.

Question 6. If you do try to modify your accent, to what extent have you been successful?
Can you, for instance, 'turn on' a Standard English accent whenever you want to?

All the people who said they tried to modify their accent believed that they had been successful and that they could quite easily speak in a Standard English accent whenever they got into the right environment. Some said that they modified their accent quite subconsciously at times when they were conversing with someone who spoke 'well'—more females than males.

Question 7. Where do you think your attitudes toward accent were formed (e.g. school, parents, work)?
Were they very heavily influenced by teachers?

Most of the older people admitted that their teachers had made great attempts to make them 'talk proper' and made them feel guilty about their accents. People of my generation said that the influence had transmitted itself to their parents who told them

54

that their mode of speech was lazy and slovenly and threatened them with elocution lessons.

The answers to this questionnaire illustrate at first-hand how difficult it is to be objective towards one's own language and, indeed, other people's, and also the difficulty of judging one's own language behaviour accurately. As Labov discovered about New York, and Peter Trudgill in Norwich,[3] people have relatively little notion of how they actually speak, and one might take a questionnaire such as this one much further. It would be possible to do an entire language project in the area of dialect on language attitudes.

If, then, we have seemed unduly discouraging as to studying dialect, it is perhaps because we have so often seen projects which exemplify one or several of the pitfalls which we've mentioned. If the student or pupil has the initiative to obtain a substantial and original text or texts and if he is aware of the possible difficulties involved in analysis, then dialect can be a fruitful and worthwhile area of study.

I do feel that the task I set myself has been successfully accomplished in many aspects. I did find myself what I feel to be an adequate text, and I feel that it reveals a lot about the village and the villagers themselves. In carrying out this language study I have discovered much of which I was previously unaware. I had accepted quite passively the language of my home life, and it wasn't until I had come to look at it objectively, and tried to define as many words and phrases as I could, that I became fully aware of its true existence.

In carrying out this study, I have come to know a great many people better than I ever thought was possible, and I have come to realise how important a language is in such a small community. It has forced me to become aware of communication in a language form, and to become equally aware of how language varies throughout the land. Each area will speak a basic English language, but in reality every one has its own individual dialect.

Register

As we said earlier, the term 'register' has accumulated among linguists and language teachers a very wide range of definitions. At its broadest, it encompasses something like all of language interaction, including written forms as well as spoken. We have deliberately narrowed our interpretation of register in the projects which we have selected as samples, largely because we feel the focus they take—on occupational language—is a useful one for language study. This is not to discount register in a larger sense, as will be illustrated presently in the study of Irish horse enthusiasts, but rather to make our starting point something feasible and fairly simple. We've chosen a Lincolnshire shipsmith, a Staffordshire farrier, and an Irish horse enthusiast as examples, but the possibilities are very numerous, and we've had language projects devoted to teachers, hippies, market-stall holders, bookmakers, charladies, military personnel, doctors and taxi drivers.

In varying degrees, dialect is likely to play a part, and our sample students all identified their subject's language with a particular place. Obviously, in certain other occupations this might be much less the case. If the project is focusing on the language of a single individual, idiolect also becomes a consideration, as indeed it did in the area of dialect study. That students often confuse these overlapping areas has already been mentioned, and, ironically, in our three sample projects, the student who best separates them is the one who uses the least terminology.

After a brief section on the Lincolnshire dialect in very general terms, the first student describes her participant's background:

Background of the shipsmith
The subject is 74 years of age and was born in Lincoln in 1898 where he attended the St. Andrew's Church of England School. He is the only survivor of a family of seven and his father was a cobbler; his mother died just after the second world war; his father died ten years ago.

In 1914 when he was sixteen he went to work as a smith for Roby's of Lincoln, making threshing machinery for Russia. The firm, however, went bankrupt as a result of Russia's not paying her debts but by this time war had been declared and he went into the marines for nine months after lying about his age.

After returning home he found jobs were scarce and worked on and off for three months as a farm labourer. He then managed to get a job as a shipsmith with Clark and Co. on Grimsby Fish Docks, where he worked for forty-eight years.

He is characteristically a very jovial character and his language is occasionally very coarse. Sometimes his speech has a tendency to be inarticulate because he may talk exceedingly quickly about

56

something that may interest or excite him; but on the other hand, in general conversation his speech is slow and clumsy. Because the subject I was interviewing was ill at ease it was difficult for him to speak naturally but because he began talking about life at work which is his chief interest, he tended to talk rather quickly and all the conversation could not be recorded.

This is a useful beginning, if a little sketchy. The student focuses her project on a text, in the form of a transcript of a taped interview, from which she extracts material for analysis of phonology, grammar and vocabulary. Here is a part of her text:

Then we did three link chains for navy for government; don't know what they was for; we made shackles for mines... anyway after war we started making anchors using electric welding... we had been using fire before to do it... now they make hundred pound apiece trawl doors but stern fishers is important now, altogether different... Casalt firm employed us a lot... all kinds of stuff is sent away and you get stuff from them there Midland factories to make up and put together... we had some laughs you know with new boys. We stuck them on blocks with nails to initiate them.

In her section on grammar, she makes the following comments on this passage, which provides a good illustration of a common misunderstanding:

His speech is confusing because of the omission of the adjective 'the' especially where he talks of making 'three link chains for navy for government'. What he meant in this instance was that the government ordered three link chains to be manufactured for use by the navy.

A person not used to hearing about the subject's life on the docks, or who knew very little about trawling would not comprehend the first few lines beginning 'now they make hundred pound....' The interpretation of this is that the firm makes 'trawl doors' which cost about a hundred pounds each; they are necessary because stern fishing trawlers are important now, so the work is altogether different from what it has been in the past.

Here is a student who does not really understand what register is and who also fails to appreciate its relationship to dialect. The omission of the definite article and the use of the nominal group 'hundred pound apiece trawl doors', in which 'hundred pound apiece' is used as a modifer, are grammatical features, not sources of confusion. Indeed, to a listener unfamiliar with the sound patterns of the Lincolnshire dialect, the tape recording itself may well be difficult to understand, but in the transcript what the shipsmith means is perfectly clear. What is required is an analysis of grammatical features, not a paraphrase of meaning. As in several other examples, this student's pre-occupation with 'correctness' gets in the way of her analysis and prevents her from seeing what is in the text.

In addition, the conclusion of this particular study also illustrates the prejudices and entrenched social attitudes to language which students often hold.

Environment and background have obviously affected the language of this Lincolnshire shipsmith. Better educational facilities nowadays give better opportunities for language. The subject received little schooling and so his language development suffered, with the result that individual words are not pronounced very well and his speech is, generally speaking, inarticulate to people not from the Lincolnshire regions; but it has some similarity to the Yorkshire dialect and people from that region would be aware only of an accent rather than the inaccuracies in his speech.

The environment also obviously contributes to the language development of a person. He has had the experience of coming from a town the size of Lincoln, not particularly large, and working with people from a similar background. This may have had a detrimental effect on his language as there are not many opportunities for different types of conversation in the various types of situations.

Here the student is aware of a connection between language and 'environment', but the use she makes of her awareness is revealing of her own attitudes. Like the previous student, her tone is even more clearly pejorative, with such phrases as 'not pronounced very well', 'inaccuracies in his speech', 'a detrimental effect', and her contention that in a town the size of Lincoln and working with people from a similar background, 'there are not many opportunities for different types of conversation in the various types of situations'. A commentary such as this not only illus-

58

trates the difficulties many, if not most, students have in being objective about language—or even recognizing that they are not being objective—but provides a starting point for further exploration concerning the social nature of language.

The next student, describing the speech of a Staffordshire farrier, displays a similar attitude.

Due to his work, he is taken to the upper class homes in the area, where he meets people with cultured and intellectual accents. These are largely the owners of race-horses, and to homes where horses can be afforded as a hobby. This again, is slowly affecting his accent, along with the fact that one of his closest colleagues at work is Polish. All of these are bound to be influencing factors in his language patterns.

He is very fond of using long and complicated words, an example being 'approximately' as can be heard in the tape extract. These sound quite foreign in his normal speech, but have obviously been experienced at some time, probably in this upper-class setting, as mentioned. I also found that when I was interviewing him, he tended to imitate the type of language heard in these settings, at first, with a widespread use of these more cultured words.

Here register in its broader sense is evident. The student senses that the language of the farrier changes in a recorded interview situation, though his description of such changes is imprecise. His transcript, too, provides an interesting illustration both of the register of a certain occupation and also of register switching. (This is much more evident on the tape itself when the farrier's voice can be heard in marked variation.)

(a) (*sounds of filing, pounding, neighing of horses throughout*)
This is a young horse. It's never had any shoes on before, so we've got no old shoes ta take off. All to do this time is dress the foot, shape it level, free from all bits of grit, stones, anything that might be bedded in the foot before we fit the shoe. Whoa. Shoeing a young horse like this, got t' have plenty patience—and tact. What you can hear now is the rasping down the foot. Whoa, whoa, whoa, bairn. Talk to the horse—it sometimes gives 'em confidence. Whoa, whoa! Let the foot rest. See what the shoe looks like. Come, come on, come on now. Whoa! Whoa there, bairn.

Whoa there, pretty. That's the shoe nearly fitted now. We'll just level it up and we've nearly done. Whoa, whoa, whoa. What you can hear now is the nail being driven into the horse's foot. Whoa, whoa, whoa, my girly.

(b) I attended Ruffclose Primary School until the age of five. I lived approximately four mile from the school and I'd to walk both ways there and back each day. I can remember taking a fishing rod many a time, bobbin' school, and goin' fishing. This I used to enjoy very, very much. I used to enjoy the countryside round there. It was lovely—the green fields, the corn fields, the hedges, beautiful in the summer. Winter—all covered in snow. I've walked to school through two foot of snow and thought nothin' of it— really enjoyed it, as all the children used to do. We left there, as I say, when I was about five. Because of this was to be nearer to my father's work, who was a blacksmith farrier. . . .

My job in those days was to take the shoes off the horses, dress the feet; when I say 'dress the feet' I mean prepare the feet for the new shoes that were to be fitted. My father's job was to fit the new shoes and then my job was to nail them on, and then up to him to finish off and clinch up. Other than the shoeing we had approximately four pot banks, as we used to call 'em to maintain with iron work. The hovel inside the chimney where the ware used to be fired was supported by what we termed as banding, which was a circular piece of metal approximately six inches wide by three/eights thick, going round the hovel at approximately one foot six apart. These we had to maintain and keep in good order, to keep the pot banks firing. The crown of the oven, as we used to term it, had dampers on the top. Our job was to keep these dampers in good repair and workable for the ironwork we used to do for them. This was a very, very dirty job, and I can remember working in six inches of soot, black as the ace of spades, sweating through heat from the oven underneath to get the dampers ready for the next firing. (*extract only*)

This is the kind of text which provides ample material on all levels for linguistic analysis. At its most superficial, it supplies a wealth of lexical items of the farriering trade, which the student has duly noted and defined. Looking further, one can examine the various influences, including dialect, social class, past experiences, on the idiolect of this particular farrier, which again the student attempts to do. Where the student fails is in the more difficult and subtle area of register change, which he only vaguely recognizes and never really comes to terms with. For example, although the entire text is spoken for the tape recorder in some sense, there are marked differences between (a) and (b) in the areas of (1) pausing, (2) voice pitch, (3) sentence length, (4) sentence complexity, e.g. length and number of clauses per sentence, (5) order of basic sentence components e.g. how many sentences in (a) begin with the subject as compared with (b). The student needs to ask himself the significance of this as well as what is unusual about the sentences beginning 'This I used to enjoy . . .' and 'These we had to maintain . . .' in terms of register switching.

In this sense, the project which examines the language of Irish horse enthusiasts is probably the best. Having grown up on a farm devoted to the breeding and selling of horses, the student has access to some really extraordinary source material, and she makes full use of this by recording her father during a telephone conversation, at a race meeting, selling a horse to a woman buyer, and sitting in front of the fire reminiscing with an old friend. Here is her description of her attempt to record 'a horse deal', followed by a transcription of the resulting tape.

The horse deal took place in the yard. Mrs. Frazer is an upper middle class lady who keeps a few horses in her own keen interest and her daughter's. My father has known her some time and she respects his word on the subject of horses. Mrs. Frazer has some experience of dealing. She has travelled considerably and lived in England for a year. In this instance my father was aware of the tape. As I felt sure that Mrs. Frazer would not like the idea of being recorded on tape my father consented to hiding the tape in a bag of horse brushes which he carried on his arm. The plot was highly successful and I consider my father very natural on the tape.

Mrs. F.	Good morning, Mr. Patterson. How are you?
Dad	Good morning, Mrs. Frazer.
Mrs. F.	Eh, I've bin thinking of buying myself a horse. Would you 'ave anything in a show hack for sale?
Dad	Ah have. Aye, I can sell you a nice little grey hack by Prince's Brew out of a dam with a string of championships to her credit. He's a gelding, four year old.
Mrs. F.	Has he done anything?
Dad	He was second at Royal Dublin the first time showed and is a hack with extravagant movement and

	excellent temperament; quality little horse that will go right tae the top and is definitely good enough to win Wembley in the right hands.
Mrs. F.	Well, I would be interested to see him. He sounds that he might suit my job all right, but maybe he would be on the expensive side for my means. Could you give me some idea of the price?
Dad	Well, I'll, I'll say you should have a luck at him and if you think of having a deal, I won't be too hard on you.
Mrs. F.	Fair enough, Mr. Patterson, eh. We'll have a look at him. Would you mind bringing him out?
Dad	Fetch out that grey hack, Joe.

(*Next we hear Joe, the groom, bringing out the horse and walking him about.*)

Dad	Stand him up on his legs there, Joe. Back a step. There now, how's that for horseflesh, Mrs. Frazer? D'you like him? Give us a few yeards of a trot there, Joe. Good mover isn' he.
Mrs. F.	Just walk him away there, Joe, and trot him back again. Could you do that again, Joe, there. Just I, I just missed seeing him coming down there right. Come on.
	Yes, that looks all right, Mr. Patterson.
	He's quite nice, eh. You're sure he's a four year old?
Dad	Yes, he's just four this time from foaling age. Which would be about, eh, I think he was foaled about the month of July. He was a latish foal but he's four year old, four year old this time.
Mrs. F	Well, now, could you guarantee him to be free of all vices and physically sound? I wouldn't want a horse that would give me any trouble.
Dad	Clean, clean, sound horse. No vices, no vices in or out of stable. Give him to you to be correct.
Mrs. F.	Well, now the demonstration was very satisfactory, very pleased with the horse. The only thing we have to dispute now and I hope we haven't to dispute it, would be the price. You haven't quoted me a price yet at all.
Dad	Well—
Mrs. F.	Could you give me any idea at all, like?
Dad	As long as you like the horse, we'll ask you one price for him—seven hundred and fifty pound.
Mrs. F.	You've scared me now. You, you'll talk smaller money than that now, Mr. Patterson. You'd like to

	see me with a good horse, I'm sure in the show ring. Would you consider a hundred less?
Dad	No, but I'll tell you just what I'll do with you. I'll divide a hundred, make it even money, seven hundred pound. You're free to get a vet to examine him if you feel like it.
Mrs. F.	Well, um, seven hundred you say is the price?
Dad	Seven hundred if you want 'im.
Mrs. F.	Well, I'll take a chance on it, Mr. Patterson, and I hope he's lucky to me. I like him very much. I like the look of the horse, and he shows great promise, I would say myself.
Dad	I would hope he would do well for you too.
Mrs. F.	So I'll, I'll buy the horse. I'll pay you seven hundred pounds and you'll give me a good luck penny.
Dad	Oh, there'll always be a luck penny. We'll treat you right.

Here is an extract from a text which provides a good starting point for a study of register. The student begins by listing and explaining the technical language of horse raising, e.g. 'show hack', 'out of a dam', used in the text, along with those ordinary lexical items and phrases which are used with a highly specialized meaning, e.g. 'has he done anything', 'extravagant movement', 'stand him up on his legs', 'free of all vices'. She then goes on to describe the language as it is used to make a sale and the inter-action between the dealer and the buyer which finally results in the 'horse deal' being made. This ranges from the linguistic means of arriving at the price to the rather subtle and complex use of modal auxiliaries, e.g. 'would', 'could', 'will'.

Here is a further extract of the almost Joycean dialogue which occurs between the horse dealer and his friend of many years.

The conversation between my father 'Gordon' and Barney is completely natural. It was taped in the kitchen where both of them were sitting beside the stove having a cup of tea or 'tae' as Barney would say. My mother and I were present but appeared to be busy reading. The tape recorder was concealed in the dob box beside Barney.

Barney is an Irish country man. Like my father he clearly remembers the days when transport meant horse and trap. They speak of the horse with great respect and mutual admiration. I have heard a hundred such conversations like this in our house.

63

Especially Barney does not only tell the story but relives it almost. He has always lived on a farm and the horse flesh usually meant work horses. He likes to hear of my father's success with horses in the show ring but his true love lies with the working horse and the horse in the 'olden days'. Each is an enthusiastic as the other and their expressions were full of vigour when they were telling the story. Barney's vocabulary is full of Irish expressions and dialect and my father's vocabulary is likewise affected when he is talking to him.

Barney   Well here, there's some changes the last ten years, Gordon. What has happened this last ten years in the transport an, the country's changed so much.

Gordon   Aye. They've a different way of gettin' about now from what they used to have the time that the fair used to be in Ballygawley an' Jimmy Donnelly an' Paddy Kelly used t' have their horse an' trap an' go home feelin' very merry an' feelin' maybe that merry that they weren't able for t' sit up in the trap, they'd be lyin' drunk in the...

Barney   As ya mention Jimmy Donnelly I remember one night an' there was a crowd of us around Killeeshie Bridge. Well, Jimmy came along wi' this big mare, big Maggie he called her. She was a great trotter. She went with a sort of three legged gallop. Jimmy was commin' along, an' he was lyin' at his length in the bottom of this trap an' him paraletic drunk an' there was a coat of snow on the ground, you know, an' we were lyin' about the crossroads. One o' the lads gathered up a snowball and he hit Jimmy just across the butt o' the ear. An' Jimmy wakes up, says Jimmy, 'If I can get at yiz, I'll cut the head a' yiz.' Jimmy jumps outa this bogey an' he had the loadin' butt an' he after us, but we snowballed away at 'im. Anyway he had to go on at the finish. He niver got near us. But ah now, there were some wonderful times them times. Paddy Kelly too would come home tight and he had a wee mare. This wee mare would trot home the whole road if he was, if he had twenty mile t' go. An' she would take every corner be'd sharp or, no matter what it was like she niver would...

Gordon   Make a miss.

Barney   Niver would make a miss. She would land till her own yard. Aw now its wonderful times now there, there wasn't as many accidents on the road that time as is now.

Gordon	Oh now the horse, he, he was still intelligent.
Barney	The horse was still intelligent.
Gordon	What about the time that Donnelly went up round t' Crossleys that the . . .
Barney	Aye, the horse, an' there was a fall of snow on the ground that time too, an' the horse got lost in the snow and he turned up, instead a' turnin' up at Killymaddy Bridge he turned up a bit soon an' turned up at Crossleys' gatelodge. He turned up the avenue or walked away up to the house up the avenue an' turned left in along the pond and walked t' the far side of the pond and a' suppose he discovered that he was wrong an' he turned, he wheeled round t' the right an' came back out on the avenue and down to the main road an' turned right and landed him home.
Gordon	Safe and sound.
Barney	Safe and sound and him lyin' drunk in the bottom o' the trap. Aw, but the type a people ya have now, Gordon, the' wouldn't know the first thing. The' wouldn't know how to put harness on a horse.
Gordon	They'd hardly know.
Barney	Nor the' wouldn't know what rein t' pull t' drive him hardly.
Gordon	Some o' them wouldn't.
Barney	Some o' them wouldn't.
	. . . . . .
Barney	. . . We started in both roads, that was about one o'clock in the day an' ploughed then till night up and down, an' there wasn't a wet hair on her. She was, y'know one o these piebald hardy ones.
Gordon	Aye.
Barney	But there's many a siege the men come through wi' horses.
Gordon	Oh many a one.
Barney	Oh God save us.
Gordon	Many a one.
Barney	Many a siege.

This is not only fascinating material in itself, potentially a text which can be analysed on all linguistic levels, but also clearly illustrates the switching of register referred to earlier. Perhaps because the student is so familiar with her material and her participants as well, she picks this up with perception.

65

It is very interesting when we compare my father's spoken language to Barney and his language when speaking to Mrs. Frazer. When he is speaking to Barney, they share the same dialect. My father drops the ends of words, especially ending in 'ing' and uses 't' instead of 'to' and 'an' instead of 'and'. With Mrs. Frazer his vocabulary is more elaborate and he mostly finishes off his sentences. As Mrs. Frazer is a very educated and refined Irish lady, I think this had a bearing on his conversation. It is also very noticeable that his choice of words has a bearing on the fact that he wants to sell the horse. Words such as 'quality', 'sound', 'correct', and 'excellent' support this. The fact that my father ignores her remarks about the price until she has seen and liked the horse also point out that he has considerable knowledge of breeding, and knows Mrs. Frazer and her ways.

During the conversation with Barney, it is noticeable that both of them have a habit of repeating what they themselves have just said to the other. Sometimes one finishes off what they know the other is going to say. An example of this is when my father says 'make a miss' and Barney repeats it. This shows that both parties are engrossed in the conversation.

But here again although the student perceives the register change, she has not gone nearly far enough in detailing its actual occurrence, though of course this is only a small part of her commentary. By and large, it is probably most difficult to get students to explore their material fully. With register, whether the focus is occupational language or something else, the student must take care to be precise within the limits of his capabilities, must use his initiative to collect enough material and, once he has collected a text or texts, to examine it in detail. The tutor can help a great deal here by a preliminary tutorial after the material has been collected, showing the student how to approach it and forcing him to go beyond generalities. All of the projects quoted in this chapter illustrate this need, just as they also illustrate the capacities of most students, when pushed, to come up with interesting and varied textual material.

Idiolect

P.H.   What first gave you the idea to take in students?
Mrs. S.   Well / it wasn't idea at all / er / yer know ow I do dress-makin' / one o me freners came to ave a / yer know / dress fitted / an she'd always done students ever since

they'd / er / started the College / and er / she said the'
were des'pret for / er / you know / students / er / lodgin'
/ an she got two students what's freners was in some
digs at West Bridgford which wasn't very nice / er /
I think the' were cold an damp / one o these attic type
o rooms / an the' were desp'ret to find some digs on
the estate / an she knew I'd got a empty bedroom which
ad got / which was already furnished wi' twin beds /
an she asked me if I'd like to take them on / an we
said / oh / we don't know / because er / it does take
a little bit o thinkin' about / an er / we left it about
a week and then I rang er up an said we'd try it / well
/ then it came to / these girls 'ad already fount somewhere / but / er / the lodgin' officer at the time 'eard
about that I said I would and came to visit me an told
me all the details about it / an er / yer know / that /
er / if we fount wasn't suited or satisfied or anythink
/ as long as we gave them a notice / a week's notice
/ this would be accepted / yer know / just for a trial
/ an er / then we ad them in the September....

How then does focusing on idiolect differ from on dialect or
register? Idiolect is in many ways the most straightforward way to
approach a text such as this one, a transcript of a tape recording
of the speech of a Nottingham landlady. Although the same linguistic levels which have been discussed in the previous sections
are still relevant, the emphasis is a different one. Here is the
student's analysis on one aspect of phonology—the pronunciation
of certain sounds and sound patterns—based on this text.

As I mentioned earlier, when I began to look closely at the transcript of the recording, I realised that there were not as many
differing pronunciations as I had noticed in Mrs. Smith's everyday conversation. However, the transcript contains some
pronunciations which I think are worthy of notice.
  The first one that occurs is where 'difficulty' is pronounced 'dif-
ficulte'. This appears to be a fairly regular variation of Mrs.
Smith's idolect, as she says 'lonele'. All words which are
pronounced by most people as ending with a 'y', Mrs. Smith con-
verts to an 'e' ending. For example, she says my own name as
'Pegge', 'family' becomes 'fam'le', 'properly' is pronounced
'prop'le' and 'memory' as 'mem're'.
  'Student' is pronounced 'stoodent' whereas the Everyman's

67

English Pronouncing Dictionary, compiled by Daniel Jones, gives the R.P. of 'student' as 'stju:dent'. Likewise 'new' is pronounced 'noo' instead of the R.P. version of 'nyu.' These are akin to American pronunciations and appear to be quite common in the Nottingham area.

We find Mrs. Smith's first contraction on the tape when she pronounces 'regular' as 'reg'lar', whereby omitting the vowel 'u'. This is perhaps a convenient moment to look at Mrs. Smith's contractions and see how she omits syllables and vowel sounds in various words. Examples of this occur with the word 'family'; Mrs. Smith misses out the vowel 'i', thus making the word 'fam'le'. Again, 'different' is pronounced 'diff'rent' and 'desperate' is pronounced 'des'pret', 'properly' becomes 'prop'le', 'memory' becomes 'mem're', 'actually' is turned into 'ashley' and 'listening' is pronounced 'lis'nin'.

Sometimes, two words are slurred; for example, 'going to' is said as 'gonna', and 'according' becomes 'cordin', which leads to the interesting question of where the 'g' on the end of 'ing' words is dropped and where it is kept. I can, in fact, find in the transcript no instance where the 'g' is clearly pronounced so that words become, for example, 'avin', 'bein', Boxin', 'actin', etc. An interesting exception to this rule is the way words ending with 'thing' are pronounced. Always, both on and off the tape, Mrs. Smith says 'somethink', 'anythink', and 'nothink'. This is done irrespective of the letter immediately following and is a characteristic I have noticed in the speech of many Midlanders and Northerners, particularly some Lancashire people.

In the same way that the end of 'thing' is pronounced 'k', so the last letter of the word 'found' is changed into 't'. This is a regular occurrence throughout the tape; ''e fount she'd', 'man fount a way' and 'fount somewhere'. Although I conjectured at an early stage that 'fount' was said when it was followed by the word 'that' and that it was an elision. However, 'fount a way' is not a shortened version of 'found that a way' and, when I asked Mrs. Smith to say the word later, she said a very definite 'fount'.

The most noticeable and to me most fascinating of the traits of Mrs. Smith's accent is her treatment of diphthongs. As it was the very first thing I noticed when she first spoke to me, I am still surprised when she splits up various words into more syllables than is usual. To begin with, I thought this to be an indiscrimate selection of words, but after a fairly close examination of the transcript and listening more intently to Mrs. Smith's voice, I have realised that there are indeed patterns which decide when a diphthong is split and when it is not.

On the tape, Mrs. Smith says 'e-at', 'we-ek', 'bedro-om', 'trees', 'spe-ak'. Others that I have noticed are 'ei-ight', 'to-ast', 'ro-ad', 'stra-ight', 'he-at', 'bre-at'. An interesting point is that Mrs. Smith also pronounces 'brake' as 'bre-ak', thereby indicating that she has heard the word 'brake', associated it with 'break', and diphthonged it accordingly. Another unusual aspect is the pronunciation of 'friends', which is something like 'freners'.

Words which Mrs. Smith does not split up are 'group', 'really', 'pronouncing', 'about', 'details', 'teaching', and 'people'. Mrs. Smith also tends to split up words which are not necessarily containing diphthongs. For example, she says 'o-am', for 'home', 'ri-at' for 'right', 'ga-et' for 'gate', 'ca-ek' for 'cake', 'pla-et' for 'plate', 'esta-et' for 'estate', 'ow-en' for 'own', 'Chin-ears' for 'Chinese', 'ro-ers' for 'rows' and 'flow-ern' for 'flown'.

I would have put forward two possible explanations for this facet of Mrs. Smith's idiolect. Firstly, it is a trait of Nottingham people to split diphthongs, particularly the women who have experienced working in lace factories. This may be due to the intense noise of the machinery and the necessary shouting that is the only way one may be heard above the noise of the machinery. It is more difficult to say a single syllable when the voice is raised and be understood than it is when speaking in a normal voice.

Secondly, when I made enquiries about the way Mrs. Smith was taught to read, I was not surprised when she told me that, during the disruption of her school life due to the Second World War, she did most of her very early reading alone and that to work out what particular words were she would block different sounds off and then put them together to make the word. So, if we take a word such as 'break', we can see that theoretically it says 'bre-ak'. When there was no teacher to correct this pronunciation, the habit may have been carried on.

For pronunciation, there are no other large aspects to describe except for a few common ones found in many Nottingham people. Among these is the conversion of 'nothing' to 'noert', 'anything' to 'oert' and 'make' into 'mek'. Similarly, 'faultless' is pronounced 'foteless'.

A number of points are worth commencing on in this analysis. First of all, this student is not looking for the features of the Nottingham dialect, though these inevitably enter in, but the idiosyncrasies, so to speak, of the language of Mrs. Smith. She is attempting to discriminate, to define those features of pronunciation which make the speech of Mrs. Smith individual, even unique. In order to do this, she relates the background of her participant to her pronunciation of diphthongs in a rather ingenious way. Even though this is pure conjecture and unsubstantiated, it does demonstrate an awareness of the social and environmental aspects of language which students often lack and which on the whole should be encouraged.

The student is also aware of the local dialect and attempts to separate as best she can the features which are a part of that dialect from those individual to Mrs. Smith. Her perseverance with the pronunciation of 'found' is interesting, even though she fails to generalize from her finding or to take it any further. Also, her analysis demonstrates a certain confusion about the relationship between orthography and speech which is very common, as in paragraph four with her description of words like 'family', 'different', 'desperate' and 'memory'. She describes Mrs. Smith as 'missing out vowels' in her pronunciation of these words when in fact the vowels are present in orthography only, and indeed we all commonly say 'des'pret' and 'diff'rent', etc. This is perhaps not only an attempt to relate pronunciation too closely to spelling but also a result of one of the most common attitudes to language—that most speech is somehow lazy, that the sound patterns of less prestigious dialects are the inevitable product of sloth rather than historical antecedents. (Note the questionnaire on Cockney English, in which 78% of persons asked felt that their particular form of speech was 'lazy'.) Still, one ought not to be over-critical, and this type of analysis seems to us an example of what we can reasonably expect from students at this stage. If there are certain difficulties with the detail of the phonological transcription, it is on the whole quite comprehensible and even at times insightful. The student has listened with evident care and interest, and she goes on to describe Mrs. Smith's grammar, vocabulary and other features of phonology.

To give one further example of idiolect, one of the areas most often chosen by our students for study is the language of small children. Many students have access to a small child and have become aware of that child's gradual mastery of speech and his remarkable ability to communicate from a very early age. In one sense, a young child usually proves to be an excellent subject for a language project because the features which differentiate his language from the 'norm' are marked ones and, on a superficial level, easy to identify if not to describe. Also, what he has to say is often interesting and amusing, though trying to record a small child's speech is not without its problems, as the following passage attests:

70

As can be imagined, there are many problems in taping a small child's speech, and with Neil I couldn't use the microphone without him noticing, as unlike the child in Andrew Wilkinson's book, he never once thought it was a vacuum cleaner! Often I heard him say things that were just made to be recorded. But did I have my equipment?—No! Besides, the inspired utterances were usually made amidst the general babble and chatter of the tea-table, or the joyful shouts of a full-scale, action-packed adventure, so that such gems as 'Gi' me a dwink, pal, I bin ridin' 'froo deser' fur twenty-forty days' were missed, or things like 'Gi' me that or I'll bash 'oor face in' were howled down by adult members of the family as being 'no way for a small boy to talk' or 'You can't use THAT, John,' and when played back sounded like the annual monkey's tea-party at the zoo! At last I had him to myself one morning, while Mum went to the shops. He was not in the right frame of mind. 'But I want to go to the shops too,' he screamed for ten minutes. Two Opal Fruits later, peace reigned; all was silence. But I didn't want silence, I wanted speech. I turned on the television. 'Visual stimulus,' I thought cunningly, turning the sound down after ten minutes. No comments were forthcoming, except a demand to turn it back on. It soon became a case of blackmail. 'I'll speak if you let me see the television.'

Under these circumstances the language I got was not the language I wanted. Rather he said things to get me and the recorder out of the way, and his responses were prompted by my questions.

In another sense, however, describing the idiolect of a child is an extremely difficult task, especially if the description is to operate on all levels: the grammatical, phonological, lexical and semantic. This is particularly true when the student chooses a child of two and a half or more, when many children have mastered the grammatical structures and systems to such an extent that they are verging upon the adult model. Writing a grammar for such a child becomes an impossible task, and we usually suggest that a student select some particular feature or features of the child's grammar to concentrate on. For example, one student elected to examine the child's use of 'functors', i.e. prepositions, pronouns, articles and conjunctions. Certainly this would suit only the more sophisticated student, and one would not in any case expect the complexity and detail of a volume on linguistics.

Another student might choose to concentrate on questions, both in terms of grammatical form and also to the extent that they reveal the child's capacity to engage in conversation, which would include his responses to the questions of others as well as his ability to ask them. This is an interesting area, though whether students should be encouraged to select it depends to a large extent on the texts or texts they are able to collect. Obviously, a text containing only a few questions is not going to prove very fruitful in this area. One other aspect of a child's language which has interested some students is the idea of 'imitation', though these students require some discussion with the tutor and some background reading in order to come to a working definition of imitation before they begin. Once again, this is a difficult area, and the most comprehensive study of acquisition, Roger Brown's *A First Language*, will probably be a challenge to even the most able of students. However, this is not to say that students can achieve nothing by working intuitively on a text of a small child. Here is a brief excerpt from a text collected by one student and his comment on that particular exchange:

Mother	Yes—I think it was the chimney smoke on a walk yesterday—we saw the chimney smoke didn't we.
Simon	Chimney smoke—walk.
Student	On a walk—where did you go.
Simon	The pussies. (?)
Student	To the bushes?
Simon	Uh—no—er
Mother	Where did we go Simon.
Simon	Uh—pussies—the pussies.
Mother	See the pussies?
Simon	Uh—no—the pussies—a puss—cat sleep—Katy's sleep.
Student	Do we have to be quiet.
Simon	Mmm—Katy's sleep.
Mother	Katy's the baby next door—she's asleep.
Simon	Katy go walk.

The limited nature of the text makes it difficult to draw any firm conclusions about the importance of imitation, except to note that it does occur. However, the evidence of Simon's insistence on making his meanings clear indicates that his language is not bound by a stimulus-response pattern. He shows signs of wanting to produce speech for which he is not yet fully equipped. On one occasion he was particularly frustrated by his lack of words and structures and experienced difficulty in making us understand what he was saying. This occurs on the last page of the transcript and concerns the 'pussies'. I have transcribed this utterance as 'pussies' although after several hearings I am not absolutely sure that it is not 'bishes' or 'pushes' (related to Katy being taken for a walk). In this conversation Simon resisted all attempts at translation and only seemed satisfied when he had told us that Katy was asleep and had gone for a walk. It is impossible to decide what sequence of thoughts were prompting his words here but it was evident that he was striving to convey some meaning to two apparently obtuse adults, and our attempts to help were of no use. The point of this is that the suggestion that language is acquired mainly through imitation seems too passive a theory to account for the drive and need for speech which occurs in children.

In this instance one feels that the student's 'intuitions' are leading him in the right direction, and that one might easily build on these intuitions and develop them further. Whether or not this is feasible depends largely on the kind of course the student is pursuing and the nature of the educational institution he is a member of. Perhaps he will be offered further courses in language study, even in linguistics, and if so then such a project as this provides a useful introduction. But, to those students, who may well be in the majority, for whom the language project provides his only real experience of 'studying language' in a formal sense, the following comments have a special relevance. First of all, having looked at Roger Brown and others in relation to his own text, this student concludes that:

Because Simon did not appear to fit into the pattern of indices which Brown uses to differentiate the stages I felt it was wiser to examine and describe his language under a series of simple headings, drawing on other sources where necessary or helpful. In other words it seemed wiser and safer to work out my own simple methodology than to try and force my text into the framework of the 'expert' investigations.

If this way of proceeding is more 'safer' than 'safe' (and we hope we have not minimized its dangers), it does force the student to think for himself, throwing him back on his own resources and latent knowledge of language. This student goes on to say that, however, the most interesting discovery has been that even from so small a text a wealth of information is apparent,

which is precisely what we are trying to get students to see, from whatever angle they approach this 'information'. But his final comment seems to us the most significant and a fitting way to end this chapter:

But the major conclusion I draw personally from the task of making an examination such as this is an appreciation of the complexity of the process of language acquisition, and an appreciation of how little it is possible to 'know' and how much has to be tentatively inferred.

4 Interaction

Interaction has been approached from a number of differing perspectives and by means of several disciplines, including linguistics, psychology, sociology and education. Obviously, if explored in depth from any of these perspectives or a combination of them, it can become very technical and complex, well beyond the capacities of the beginning student. However, in terms of gathering source materials, students find it among the most fruitful and rewarding language areas for a number of reasons: (1) Its importance and relevance to the activities of everyday life are easy to recognize, and only recently being fully explored; (2) Interesting texts are usually accessible without too much difficulty; (3) Ordinarily these texts lend themselves to analysis without the use of a model too complicated for the student to understand and apply; (4) There are a number of books available which offer a certain amount of guidance should the student feel the need[1] (though none of the three projects cited in this chapter actually makes use of these).

Perhaps we should define more closely what we mean by interaction. In the first place because we are members of an English Department and this is a *language* project, our emphasis is necessarily on the linguistic features of any text. We encourage the students to analyse the actual language used by the participants. Hence such topics as social background and its implications, the psychological states of the participants, pedagogical assumptions and judgments must be brought in where relevant but should not provide the focus for the study, something not always easy to get across to the student, as he tends to find these aspects considerably easier to deal with than the language itself. Paralinguistic features, such as gesture, eye contact, dress, movement and spacing, are also significant but seldom provide satisfactory focal points.

75

Students should be made aware of their existence and importance but would find it extremely difficult to analyse them in detail.

John Sinclair in *Towards an Analysis of Discourse* asks the following questions, which provide a convenient starting place for looking at a text: 'What function does a given utterance have—is it a statement, question, command or response—and how do the participants know; what type of utterance can appropriately follow what; how and by whom are topics introduced and how are they developed; how are "turns" to speak distributed and do speakers have differing rights to speak.' We would, however, suggest using Sinclair's actual model only with the really exceptional student, as it is too complex for most of our first year students to apply without great difficulty. In any case, the model as it stands applies to classroom interaction and would need considerable modification if one were to tackle a different situation or even the usual infant school classroom.

Also in this area we tend towards focusing on interaction in the more structured situations, which can range from any type of classroom to committee meetings, interviews and the Courts. Casual conversation and phatic communion present slightly different problems and have in any case been discussed earlier. Sinclair's questions become increasingly less difficult to answer as the situation which produces the interaction becomes itself more structured.

For example, here is a part of the text taped by a student in an infant school classroom. The school is in an educational priority area; the teacher is sitting on a chair with some twenty-five children grouped on the carpet at her feet; she is talking about 'People Who Help Us', a topic which has been discussed previously with the class on a number of occasions.

Teacher	We've got a picture here—look—of a nurse.
Robert	She's taking the lunches round.
Teacher	Yes she's taking the lunches round.
George	She's er—she's er—she's er . . .
Teacher	What's that she's got on?
Keith	What's that dinner Miss?
Leonard	A cap.
Teacher	She's got a white cap on—what else has she got on?
George	Er . . .
Mandy	A uniform.
Teacher	A uniform.

Mandy	Yeh.
Teacher	That's right—a uniform.
Keith	Miss what they having for dinner?
Teacher	And all—and all the people.
Keith	Fish and chips.
Teacher	No it's not fish and chips—I don't think—all the people we've talked about so far.
Leonard	It's ham and potatoes.
Teacher	Have got uniforms on haven't they—the policeman has a blue uniform and the fireman has a blue uniform.
Leonard	They have red ones.
Teacher	And the postman has a blue uniform.
Keith	It's black—Miss I'm gonna kill that postman.
Teacher	And this nurse has got a blue uniform on hasn't she?
Robert	(*laughs*)
Teacher	And I wonder who she's taking the dinner to—I wonder what's the matter?
Robert	The patients.
Teacher	Yes the patients.
Keith	She's taking it to the king.
Teacher	And look at the picture of the patients in hospital.

This example is only a small part of the complete text, and the student has previously discussed such features as patterns of inter-action, types of questions and responses, the role of the teacher and the nature of the larger and immediate situation. She goes on to describe the teacher's aim in this particular sequence.

The teacher's aim is to discuss exactly what can be seen on the picture of the nurse who is bringing the patients their dinner. Above all she wishes to relate past lessons on 'People Who Help Us' to the nurse and chooses the nurse's uniform as the link. Robert establishes that 'She's taking the lunches round' and then the teacher attempts to find out from the children what the nurse is wearing. But Keith is not satisfied and decides to use his imagi-nation. He wants to know what the dinner is and begins to specu-late. Unfortunately for him the teacher would rather talk about the uniform. Twice he tries to interrupt. When it becomes clear he is not going to get an answer, he begins to speculate saying, 'Fish and chips'. By now Keith has managed to distract the teacher and so midway through her sentence, she breaks off to answer Keith, 'No it's not fish and chips,' but then returns to her original sentence. This is really an attempt to keep Keith quiet. The teacher cannot tell if it's fish and chips anymore than Keith can but by saying in effect 'You're wrong,' she is saying 'Be quiet.' Unfortunately this plan fails for although Keith drops the subject, Leonard also begins to speculate saying, 'It's ham and potatoes.' The teacher deliberately ignores this and finally the subject of the dinner is dropped. Why does the teacher refuse to answer Keith and Leonard? Firstly, the teacher feels compelled to keep to her lesson plan. What people eat in hospital is not among her list of priorities. Secondly, the children are deviating from what she considers to be the 'facts'. But most probably her reaction relates to Keith himself. In both lessons Keith constantly disturbs the class. The teacher is used to this and realising he wishes to draw attention to himself, has developed an automatic reaction to his interruption which results in her ignoring him altogether. Therefore even at times when he has something of value to contribute he is ignored, a reaction based on past experience.

This commentary suggests several important aspects involving interaction. First of all, the student raises the topic of 'closed questions', though she does not use that term. In other words, the teacher has a definite answer in mind, and she refuses to accept or even acknowledge responses which she considers inappropriate. Hence when Leonard responds with 'A cap' to the teacher's question, though this must clearly be an acceptable answer, it is not the one which she has in mind, and she perseveres.

Perhaps more important, the student also brings in the notion of 'illocutionary force',[2] though this is again not the term she uses. Approached as simply as possible, 'illocutionary force' involves the function of an utterance, what it *does* as opposed to what it *says*. This becomes particularly interesting when there is a disparity between the grammatical form of an utterance and its function in a particular context. Although some very complex linguistic questions arise in conjunction with the notion of 'illocutionary force', it is difficult to ignore and is in any case a fruitful area for students to explore. Another example occurs in this text when the teacher says, 'And I wonder who she's taking the dinner to—I wonder what's the matter.' The children rightly interpret this *statement* as a '*question*', and Leonard responds with the appropriate answer. Examples of 'illocutionary force' occur on nearly all tapes involving classroom interaction. *Questions* frequently perform the function of '*commands*', e.g. Will you close the window? Are you listening, Jane? Or *statements* act as '*commands*', e.g. I think
78

we should all turn to page 90. Or *questions* function as '*statements*' e.g. Didn't I say that it was John's turn next? The study of such examples is interesting in itself and can be revealing in terms of language roles in the classroom.

One of the dangers of examining classroom interaction is that of over-emphasizing the pedagogical at the expense of the linguistic or of confusing the two so that neither is clearly explored. Students find it difficult, as this student exemplifies to a degree, to look at the language of the classroom as it occurs and not to judge both the teacher and the children in terms of what he thinks they *should* be saying, but usually are not.

Objectivity becomes somewhat less difficult if a different type of situation is analysed. One possibility is the committee, and higher education being what it is, this type of language interaction is never likely to be in short supply. Any committee will provide a text such as the following, which is a transcript of part of a session of a Staff–Student Consultative Committee.

This is an interesting example, as it illustrates explicitly how a meeting which is less obviously structured than most classrooms structures itself during the course of the session. The member of staff is numbered (1), and each of the students (all male) is given a number in order to distinguish his particular utterances. The subject matter is initially the availability of reading and talking space in the Library and subsequently the question of student essays.

11	Em—and perhaps if—you know—Bill's sort of er comment holds water we can put it to other—other committees if Mr. Jones feels he doesn't want to act.
10	Well presumably each year's got one—so.
1	Yes yes they have—yeah I think—I mean he's keen I think to have an area where students can go and sit and talk—there's no opposition from librarians—just a matter of finding what—which is suitable without disturbing the facilities—so there's no resistance from him—em—side two was for your attention about the—check on the Library—er then the essays have they come back generally—em Mr. Smith I think came round and asked everyone to go and collect them—there's still quite a lot of them not been collected—er.
6	There are some still er not available for collection I understand.
2	But he does know.
6	Certain tutors haven't.
2	But he does know.

6 Yeah (*unintelligible*) that students (*unintelligible*) yeah.

4 Certain ones haven't been marked have they—they're still not there.

1 Have they not.

4 One or two haven't been marked from last year's work—when they were handed out—was it last Friday—when they were handed out.

10 Er—last Thursday.
Thursday (*a number of voices*)

4 There were some—there—that people were told that they—tutor last year hadn't marked the essay

1 Yeah—I think that's partly a function of em people leaving—er—and just leaving a little bit of unfinished work at the end of it em—I suppose if anyone's desperately keen to have it marked we'll mark 'em.

4 Do they count for anything or were they just er an exercise in writing essays?

1 Em we've had this before haven't we?

5 We've written down here—yes they do.
(*General comments all at once*)

1 This is not the—this is—that's the vacation essay—I don't think—they don't count towards the fourth year work—that last lot

11 And they were after the third years had left.

1 Yeah I—I don't know that the formal—I mean I can't give you a formal answer but I suspect they were a bit of a ...

10 Doddle.

1 Well just making the course seem more important by giving some sort of essay to begin with really.
(*General comments*)

11 Sleepless nights.

10 A window dressing.
(*General laughter*)

1 Yeah—yeah—yeah and leaving it open so that students weren't sure whether it was or not so they'd all do it anyway or virtually all do it—that's a teacher technique I suppose really you know—anyway anyone who can't get theirs knows where to go—em I've put the Honours em list up—I'm afraid rather belatedly but that people are now in the process of checking that so perhaps you would em tell your groups that it's up and it's up to them to check on their names.

7 Yeah er can I just interrupt sorry em someone asked me to ask about the vacation assignments.

2 Yes and me too.

1 All right.

On the idea of 'structuring', here is a part of the student's commentary:

For example, the staff member is not the chairman, for this Committee does not elect one and yet his command of language places him in the role of chairman. He opens the discussion, leads it to new points, refers back to certain items, decides what steps are to be taken to determine certain problems and has most questions directed at him. One person makes an apology to him for interrupting his speech yet this doesn't occur between the students. It would seem therefore that a position in authority, in some cases, is a deciding factor as to who shall command the language in a given situation; for it is a definite command that this staff member has over the meeting. Altogether he makes a total of twenty-six speeches in this extract, as compared to the next person's eighteen, which is quite a large amount considering the element of time and the size of the group.

There is a contradiction here, in that the student begins by stating that it is 'the command of language' of the member of staff which places him in the role of chairman but goes on to comment that 'a position of authority . . . is a deciding factor as to who shall command the language'. The latter seems to fit the evidence more closely, and indeed is probably true of most staff–student committees. Looking at the text more closely, we see that in terms of the number of false starts, fillers, incomplete sentences, repetitions, the speech of the member of staff is not clearly distinguishable from that of the students. However, at the level of discourse he is distinguished by those features which the student points out, though without discussing them in enough detail. Not only are his utterances more frequent than those of the students individually, they are also longer and in several instances very much longer. Also, it is interesting to examine more closely a portion of the actual interaction. There is apparently some disagreement as to whether the essays have been marked or not and (4) begins with a statement, 'Certain ones haven't been marked have they— they're still not there,' with the tag question indicating a request for confirmation and a degree of courtesy. When the tutor counters with a question, 'Have they not?' he interprets this as a request for further information and re-phrases his original statement, aided by the other students; he becomes less certain and direct. The tutor now establishes his position with his next utterance but the student persists with his question. When instead of answering the question, the tutor says, 'We've had this before, haven't we?' he clearly means that he does not wish to go into the matter, as (5) senses in his reply.

Several points can be made here. Firstly, that we now have a discussion where all the comments are being directed at the tutor, who has established himself as the nominal leader. Secondly, that if this were a classroom situation, the tutor's remark, 'We've had this before, haven't we?' would probably function as a conclusion to the discussion, as it is intended. However, given the committee situation, the students feel free to carry on, though (4) himself is silent during the rest of the tape.

The final example is outside the teaching context altogether and involves the highly structured setting of a Courtroom. Here there is no doubt about who controls the interaction, and the linguistic roles are firmly established by the situation and reinforced by the setting. The Defendent is standing in the Witness Box and the Magistrates are sitting behind a table on a raised platform. It is clearly the role of the Magistrate, aided by the Clerk, to ask questions and the Defendent has no option except to answer; neither can he interrupt or begin a new topic or bring the interaction to a close.

Clerk Yes—and what else.
Def. Um—we have a television on rental—that's one pound.
Clerk How much is that?
Def. Ten pence a week.
Clerk Is that a colour one?
Def. Yes it is.
Mag. Is that for your—?
Def. Yes that's right.
Mag. Personal use.
Def. Yes.
Mag. It is not for the client's use?
Def. Yes.
Mag. Right.
Clerk Yes.
Def. Um—I can't think of anything else.
Mag. Right.
Clerk In March you were told to pay this at the rate of two pounds a week and if you'd paid it would have I think been cleared by now.
Def. Yes it would have been—you see it's er a bit of a problem

	with this sort of thing because they—they just ring you up and expect you to be on the (unintelligible) within an hour—and er I have done jobs with these people before—then you come home and you might wait five or six weeks—and I've got an idea that because I've been inoculated to go to Ghana that they're holding me back for that particular job—it's quite an expensive business—I've had to go to London for medicals.
Mag.	Well they presumably pay the expenses.
Def.	Oh yes—they pay those—this is the thing—they've paid all this money out for me to go and then they can't get me a visa—I've the vaccination certificates here if you'd like to see them.
Clerk	Do you want to see them?
Mag.	I might as well.
Def.	That was done in June and I've been waiting ever since for a job.

The student who taped this sequence was particularly interested in the area of misunderstandings, though obviously he dealt with a number of other aspects of the text in his analysis. Here is a brief portion of his commentary:

The area to be discussed is thus the meaning of the sentences spoken, not necessarily the first level of meaning, but the concepts in the mind of the speaker as represented by his speech. This we must examine with particular reference to the institution in which the interaction took place. It would seem obvious to assume that as these individuals met at a Court to communicate they should each have appreciated the concepts the other was attempting to transmit. But was this the case? Closer analysis of part of the first case would show this assumption to be incorrect. In this instance the Defendant is explaining why he believes he will soon be going to Ghana. These lines are particularly interesting. Here the Defendant says of his having been inoculated, 'It's quite an expensive business. I've had to go to London for medicals.' The concept being expressed is hidden; the Defendant's logic, if written more fully, would be: 'Because the company has spent all this money having me inoculated, and because they do not want to waste this investment they are keeping me for this job, which is why I am still employed.' As is apparent, the Magistrate misunderstood this expression and assumed that the Defendant was making another point for inclusion in his current expenditure. Thus the reply, 'Well they presumably pay the expenses.'

The student's analysis of the misunderstanding is interesting and shows him trying to operate at the level of discourse analysis. Unfortunately, he misuses the word 'concept' in his search for adequate terminology. What he is trying to point out is that at the level of discourse the *meaning* of the sentence, 'It's quite an expensive business' is ambiguous. It can function either as a request that it be included as an item of expenditure, which is what the Magistrate assumes in the light of the previous set of utterances, or as an explanation as to the likelihood of the Defendant getting that particular job, which is what the Defendant intends, as he makes clear in his next utterance. The ambiguity occurs not in the surface structure of the actual sentence but in its function as a part of the discourse. Obviously, we could go further than this, and there are other instances of a similar kind of misunderstanding even in this tape. They illustrate very distinctly, as in fact do all the texts quoted in this chapter, the impossibility of defining the meaning of any utterance without knowing what comes before and after. 'Meaning' is so often used by students in a very restricted sense that when, as in this instance, something deeper and less obvious is clearly involved, the student feels he must grope around for another word, such as 'concept', to describe what he is talking about. Clearly, it is in this area, the realization of meanings, that a study of interaction becomes most fruitful. When the student begins to realize that meaning in this larger sense involves language on a number of levels, including phonology, lexis, grammar and context (both immediate and larger) he is gaining insight into the nature of language. He is able to see language not as something essentially static but as a process, a series of utterances which relate both backwards and forwards, only made 'fixed' by the tape recorder in the same sense that a camera captures a scene or a face at a particular moment.

Interaction is a large area, and we have managed only to cover a fraction of the total in this chapter. What we offer are suggestions, and all of these projects were much longer than the excerpts quoted. As in the other areas of language study, what is most important is to get students to make full use of their material and to explore as completely as possible the 'meaning' contained in any particular text.

5 Projects on written language

So far the emphasis in our examination of students' work has been almost entirely on projects involving a transcription of spoken texts. In fact, of all the projects our students have undertaken, perhaps half of them have been devoted to 'written' texts. If therefore we give more weight to the 'spoken' mode of language in our commentary, this reflects our belief that students are more likely to benefit in this area. Indeed, in our initial talk and subsequent tutorials we make a point of stressing to students that we tend to look more favourably on projects derived from a tape recording than on those whose text for study originated in the written mode. Our reasons for doing this are basically two. First, the greater effort needed by the student to make a recording and transcribe it not only involves him more firmly in the work but points out to him more graphically than any lecture how fundamentally different speech is from written language. In this way he immediately realizes that there is more to 'language' than he thought. Secondly, this very difference enables a student more easily to view his text from an 'outside' position. We must remember that students whose experience of language study has been limited in the school situation to O- and A-levels, with their emphasis on literature or Standard English in the written mode—with occasional sorties into advertising or newspapers—are likely to feel already when they come to us that they are competent to deal with 'language'. By bringing their previous experience to bear on texts similar to those they are familiar with they therefore give to their commentaries the kind of focus and terminology they are accustomed to use. Consequently they tend to seek out examples of 'expressive' or 'emotive' language on the one hand; and on the other to enumerate examples of images or to give a narrow and often unnecessary attention to onomatopoeia or alliteration.

This raises a fundamental issue in the whole rationale for Language Projects as an introduction to Language Study. We have to accept that the average student brings with him from his school experience a particular way of 'looking at language'. For the most part this will be of the sort described at the end of the last paragraph. Nor is there anything wrong with this in so far as it was relevant to his purposes at the appropriate time. But we view our purpose as being somewhat different. If the school focus is to use the language of a work of literature or an advertisement as illustrative of the student's own 'response' to the writing, it follows that the emphasis is not so much on the language as on something else. Essentially, the student will accept the language as aimed at *himself* as audience. What we wish to do, however, is to get the student to look at the language in such a way that the form of the language—its graphology, grammar and vocabulary—is related to the kind of audience the writer had in mind with the student himself being a third person observer of the totality. This involves a closer scrutiny of the form of the text, which is what students tend to call the 'language', as well as a more objective examination of the concept of audience. Putting it in another way, we wish the student to study the text, but no longer as the direct audience to its language. And on the whole we find that this is easier for the student if he is asked to look at the more unfamiliar type of text associated with speech rather than a text from the written mode which constantly reminds him of the kind of 'response' which he was formerly being asked to make.

As we said in the first chapter, our initial attempt to overcome this problem was to try and teach our students a linguistic model. The constant difficulty in doing this was that, with little time available for doing this thoroughly, any application of such a description to first-hand texts in such a way that it made sense to the students always seemed to fail. Above all, most of the students saw this exercise as even less relevant to their needs than the previous approach they had used in school and which, if they still studied literature, they still employed. In effect, then, the students could see little point in doing what we were asking and were bored; and this augured badly for the growth of Language Study.

In turning to the Language Project approach, and in particular to the study by the students of their own collected spoken texts, we believe we have a way out of this impasse. If too many of our students still choose written texts, at least we believe that they are more involved in the study of language than they ever were

86

before. And, of course, there are many kinds of written texts which students can explore which do not have the inherent complexity, and hence difficulty, of literature or advertising. But we shall take this up below.

First, however, a brief word about an apparent danger which the Language Project seems to have for the unsophisticated student. It will already be apparent from our comments that many of the students' commentaries on their own texts fall short of the precision and explicitness that one would wish from students of linguistics. At one level we would agree with those who might wish for a tightening up in this area. Given sufficient time with students, of course, this would not be difficult. This, within the complexities of a General Arts course, we do not have. And if we were able to offer courses of sufficient duration and rigour, we probably would not get the students. At another level we see the problem quite differently. In fact, given that the commentaries we criticize are derived from the students' own 'model-making', it could be said, not that the work lacks explicitness and precision, but that there is more of it than we could reasonably hope for. In fact, we are often surprised at the ability of some of our students to come to terms with this area of study when so much of their previous training has been in learning to perform along the lines laid down for them by their specialist teachers. Our criticisms of the work are not therefore aimed at the students themselves, but rather are meant as guidelines towards possible improvements in the various areas. They are meant to help non-specialist teachers who we hope will take up this kind of approach to Language Study in schools and colleges rather than indicate to specialist teachers of language or linguistics, who deal with students of a very different kind, where our students may have gone wrong.

But to return to our examination of projects concerned with written language. One difficulty that students find in this area, precisely because they are familiar with these kinds of texts, stems straight from that very familiarity: in using the kind of narrow focus they are used to employing they miss much that is in the text, and yet give a superficial impression of sophistication. We suggest that this problem can be avoided by a careful screening of the kind of text to be selected. For a start, we must remember that many students, having a rather narrow view of what constitutes 'language', will tend to oversimplify the divison of texts into 'spoken' and 'written' in an extreme way. On the one hand, there will be literature, which can be studied only by a 'non-linguistic' approach; and on the other, 'natural' speech, by which is meant spontaneous conversation which has to be trapped by a concealed tape recorder. Even though this is a slight exaggeration, it does represent a tendency found to some extent in most students.

One of the consequences of this is that many students, in trying to establish a text for study, feel that their choice is more limited than it need be. A frequent initial tendency is to go for a spoken text and then, when the difficulty of collecting such a text is realized, to veer towards an easily accessible text from literature. The middle ground is often overlooked.

What we propose to do in this chapter is to explore a small part of this middle ground. To do this we shall examine the work of some students who were either not put off by the difficulties above or else tried to overcome them.

First of all perhaps we should explain what we mean by a written text. In some sense every text explored by a student is a written one, since we insist that, even if the language studied was taken from a speech situation, it must first be transcribed to make it more accessible. Perhaps a useful, if vague, way of arriving at a working definition is that a written text is either one which was intended by its producer to convey its meaning primarily through the eye rather than the ear, or one which was *intended* to be read aloud by its original producer. This is not completely satisfactory, but it does include areas that share many of the characteristics of written language even though, as far as the audience is concerned, they receive the message in a spoken form. In this latter category we would put, for example, any language situation where reading aloud is found, as in many radio programmes, classroom or lecture performances, public meetings, and so on. Very similar are those contexts where a written text is learnt by heart to be spoken, or interpreted, from memory. This would include most play performances or, say, a television interview. An interesting possibility here is when the original written text can be compared with actual performances of that text, though this often presents difficulties in that untrained students will have problems in adequately describing the minutiae of pausing or intonation, or in describing the constraints imposed upon the producers of plays when they are faced with interpretative options present in an ambiguous text.

The kinds of problems thrown up by this general area of 'transmission' are explored below in the project comparing the language of a novel and a derived play. The rest of the chapter is given to exploring projects concerned with written texts in the sense mentioned above, as language conveying its message principally through the eye.

Novel into Play

The student who wanted to study the differences that occur when a text written in one genre is adapted to another chose to examine the changes made by Robert Lowell when he wrote a stage version of Herman Melville's short novel *Benito Cereno*. The study is long and detailed, and is a good attempt at this kind of project by a student who has tackled nothing of this kind before. One of his main difficulties, interestingly enough, is that, being an enterprising and perceptive student of literature, he finds his experience constantly interfering with his approach to this topic. It emerges principally in his use of the sort of comment he found useful in his literature essays:

This opening description is important and effective. Firstly there is a brilliant description of what the weather and sea were like. Everything was calm and grey. This evokes dulness and the idea of a subdued storm. And whilst undulating the sea appeared to be still which also suggests that there is an appearance of great calm and quiet but underneath there is a disquieting movement. The repetition of 'troubled grey' in connection with the birds and the elements suggests a unity between the sea and sky. The birds were skimming low in the 'grey' sky and coming in contact with the 'grey' vapours. There is a suggestion of the unity of nature and the elements to create a strong force against man. The use of similes is very apt. The birds, for example, are compared with swallows flying low over meadows before a storm. And the sea is compared to lead cooling in smelters' moulds. This is an interesting image in that something so fluid and elusive like the motion of the sea should be compared with such a rigid, cold and inanimate substance as lead. This image conjures up a picture of the molten lead flowing into the moulds and being captured there.

This is only part of a much longer paragraph about one of the earliest descriptive passages in the novel. Some of the terms used are worth noticing: 'evokes', 'the idea of', 'suggests', 'disquieting', 'appearance', and so on.

His next step is to introduce the comparable Lowell passage, which he does as follows:

Lowell's treatment of the description of the weather is in some ways different because it is written in twentieth century American whereas Melville was writing in the nineteenth century. His descriptive passage contains some of Melville's language but there are omissions and interesting words included.

After quoting the passage in question he goes on:

Lowell uses the present tense whereas Melville uses the past tense. Through Melville everything seems to be spread out in front of the reader. The author's eye is sweeping across the view and describing important aspects of the view. Lowell, however, cannot conjure up a mental picture in the same way. Through Delano (one of the main characters), we see his immediate response to what he sees. Melville's imagery suggests that some misfortune is going to occur. It is through speech and thoughts expressed verbally that Lowell can allude to some coming danger.

This exemplifies one of the prime difficulties encountered by students, that they are prone to use evaluative or evocative, but often uninformative, terms. Thus we have 'suggestion of the unity of nature' without any mention of how this effect is achieved in the writer's use of language, or indeed any question of whether this particular point is relevant to the focus of attention. We have, too, 'interesting image' with no reference to whom it is interesting, just as later we are told that there are 'interesting words included'. What is important here is that, precisely in that area where so many of the linguistic forms are included, omitted or changed because of the constraints of having two distinct audiences in the different modes, the writer of the study shows no awareness that he too is writing for an audience with a different set of expectations from those of his literature tutor. This is to suggest that the teaching of writing skills is being treated too narrowly in the sixth form.

Other phrases used liberally throughout the study include 'a flowing, artistic, linguistic style'; 'romantic style' contrasted with 'concise and plain style'; 'lyrical quality about Lowell's version'; and at the end, where an attempt is made to describe a legal document that occurs in the novel, though not the play (so that the

90

exercise is to some extent superfluous), we find 'legal language is cold and impersonal'; the 'style is impersonal'; and 'very official words'.

It is in fact singularly unfair to pick out these points for criticism in what is essentially a good study; but it is worth doing so in that they typify a widespread inability on the part of students to see the lack of specific meaning in the terms they use. Strangely enough, in this particular study, a student who is concerned to note 'Lowell's lyrical quality' omits to mention that what we have here is not merely a dramatic version of a novel, but also a poetic version of a prose original. The constraints implied by the fact that Lowell is writing a verse play are completely missed.

Indeed, it is often the simple facts that students do miss. In this study, for example, we are never given the dates of publication or presentation of the two works, but left to infer this from contextual clues about their being twentieth and nineteenth centuries. This illustrates one of the major difficulties of doing a Language Project, particularly in the written mode, and even more so when the text has literary connotations.

The second paragraph of this study illustrates both the difficulty and the advantage of never having done this sort of work before:

Before looking at the language of Melville's novel and Lowell's play, I think that it is necessary to observe that the novel and the play are completely different media. Using descriptive language Melville can set the scene and describe the characters using aspects of appearance and their mannerisms. He is able to create convincing characters in a realistic situation. Whereas Lowell relies almost entirely on dialogue to put over the situation and through their speeches we are able to discern what kind of people the characters are. He relies on props and stage directions to help to create the scene. Through description of what happens Melville evokes the atmosphere and allows the characters to develop in relation to each situation. Lowell, however, cannot set the scene. The audience plunges straight into the drama whereas the reader is led slowly into the story. The audience reacts to the visual stimulus of the stage and scenery as well as to the dialogue. The audience's response is immediate so the playwright has to create convincing characters and make the situation easily understandable. The author, however, can let things develop more slowly. He can use as much imagery as he likes and spend as much time as he likes on developing the characters, knowing that the reader can always go back and re-read any part. He has fewer restrictions than the playwright. Therefore Lowell's play deals with the same themes in a very different way. It will be necessary from time to time not only to look at the language of the novel and the play but also to mention their different ways of relating a specific situation.

What this student has seen as the main differences between the two media is summed up here very well. What he fails to do afterwards is to take the major categories he has shown to be relevant to the discussion—audience, presentation, immediacy, development, description, period of writing—and develop them in a systematic way. Instead he follows through the texts as they unfold the story. Perhaps one reason for this is the length of text he has chosen to examine, since in comparing the whole of a short novel and a play he is likely to concentrate excessively on plot and characterization and develop his work accordingly. This is why we prefer students to choose fairly short texts when doing a Language Project for the first time. For example, another student in the same area took as his text one paragraph from a novel and examined all that was involved in transferring this to the stage. It covered the same ground, but the study had much more coherence from having been given a more precise focus.

Letters

A different kind of study which has proved popular among students is the study of letters. This is a very wide field and students can make all sorts of divisions within it. A typical study of this area is worth quoting from extensively as an example of what is possible and easily within the reach of most students.

The project is entitled *A study of letters written between friends* and is organized into: Preface; Text; Introduction to the Study; Observations on individual letters; and General Conclusions. Her preface is worth quoting in full:

The first section of this study contains eleven letters written by male and female writers, some of whom are students. These letters are the text of this study.

The second section, which forms the introduction, I hope achieves the aim of awakening anyone who reads this study to the various questions everyone has asked at some time about letters. The introduction contains no presuppositions about the text, so that the observations are poignant, unprejudiced and enlightening. Some of the observations that follow are not only restricted to a study of the language used, but try also to incorporate some speculations and reasons why the language might have been used in the way it is. In doing this, and also by considering the overall 'tone' and impression created by the letters, I hope to have made a clearly signposted journey to the conclusion of the study. Observations mean little without some conclusions. Although I have incorporated conclusions with some observations, so that their meaning is clearer when juxtaposed, I also briefly remark on the findings of the whole study. The conclusion therefore deals with the similarities between and differences among the letters. Finally it is hoped that this study, whilst analysing closely nearly every sentence of the text, does not ignore the necessity for preserving its 'wholeness', and it is hoped that the letter is also seen as being a very complex work of art which, as a piece of culture and sophisticated society, is very easily influenced by a whole conglomeration of varying forces.

If we ignore the fairly obvious difficulties of expression, what emerges from this preface is that the writer has a very clear picture of what she is about. She further extends her aims and defines them more precisely in her Introduction. It is here that she shows the focus of attention she is given as well as the method for doing so. Thus she writes:

The degree of familiarity expressed in letters is most probably dependent upon the type of relationship the friends have. I shall try to discuss this also in the study. By 'familiarity' I mean not only the feelings of the writer and the recipient, but also the extent of their mutual understanding about certain points that come from their shared experience.

Having made the point that familiarity is a major category in her examination of the letters, she then tells us about the general approach she intends to use to bring this out:

Each letter is analysed separately and commented upon, and conclusions are drawn. In trying to stress the individuality of each letter, and to preserve the total impression that each letter creates, I have not grouped, say for example, all the beginnings of the

93

letters and completely detached them under a separate heading from other parts of the text. Although each letter embodies similarities and conventions, each one is different in some of the contents and the style of writing. As an interesting comparison, however, the last two letters are by the same writer.

There follows a close examination of the letters in turn. As an example, the following is the first letter of her collection, followed by the whole of her commentary on it.

Barchester 2995   14 Piltdown Mansions
                                   Barchester
Dear Jane,
    I don't how to put this. It concerns my entertainment/play/ musical, which I am pleased to say is more or less scripted. However one or two places need a little padding out. Secondly the grapevine has told me that you put up a fine performance in the camp concert, and that is what I want. I would like you to submit for inclusion that same sketch or one of a similar type, that you would perform in the entertainment.
    You would come on in Scene 4, after the hero has met with his friend. . . .
    If you want more information please don't hesitate to contact me. Apologetically I would like you to submit your script as soon as possible . . .
                    Yours
                    John Peters
                    Love & kisses

(In this letter we have changed name and address. It is important to note that the telephone number and address are printed, while the rest is handwritten.)

Observation 1   THE 'BUSINESS-LIKE' TONE
    I am not suggesting that this is a business letter, which would then raise all sorts of questions, but when I received this letter it seemed to me to be very precise and to the point. I use 'business-like' therefore to describe the style of this letter in a metaphorical sense.
    This is a close friend, who I originally only knew via a Christian Youth Organisation. Since then, the friendship has grown and
94

there have been many meetings at weekends, parties, holiday and at the 'local'.

Amongst his many social activities during his year off from University, he has tried organising plays and writing scripts for musical and dramatic evenings. As a contrast to his musical talents, his subjects have always been science-orientated. This last point is I think significant and I shall consider it again.

This letter is one of a few that he has ever had to write to me, since I normally see him frequently, and since the letter asks a favour, he was most probably a little apprehensive in writing and waiting for my reply, as I think is supported by his opening hasty sentence:

'I don't know how to put this.'

One word, 'know', is missing, suggesting perhaps that his thoughts were ahead of his pen.

Graphically, the letter appeared to be very formal, with a printed address and telephone number. As the writer sends letters so infrequently, printed titles would obviously be sensible in avoiding any confusion or ambiguity and by writing his name in full, I could then not possibly confuse him with anyone else. All these points may seem very self-evident but the writer may well have envisaged some confusion probably arising and wished to avoid this by being very specific. Besides, his letter indicates an urgency, in that he wants a script as soon as possible, and any confusions would cause unnecessary delays.

The grammar of this letter is very interesting to note. There is variety in the complicated and short sentences and he seems to use almost the technical vocabulary of those who write and produce play scripts, as for example in:

'...I would like to ask you to submit your script...'

and 'I would like to ask you to submit for inclusion...' besides his elaborated ideas:

'However one or two places need a little padding out.'

'Grapevine' is unusual but very appropriate—he has heard of my past performance in another sketch I did.

The letter is very logically set out in definite paragraphs which contain concise thoughts in each. Terms like 'secondly' channel thoughts and concentration even further. His letter is 'business-like' in that there is no 'waffle'. He explains what he is attempting to do, what he wants from me, and when, 'as soon as possible'. He elaborates only where necessary, for example in his brief description of the sequence of events in the performance.

The shortness and terseness of the letter is probably a reflection of the very precise way in which the writer thinks. Just as his letter also seems organised, so he gives the total impression that he can organise social events and the people around him. His organisation is done with considerateness, as I think is sufficiently indicated by the wording:

'Apologetically I would like to ask you to submit...'

The language of the closing greetings which interestingly come after his name, seem to soften his terseness and read as a friendly gesture. Some might consider the words to constitute a slightly modern 'trendy' convention, with close affinities with 'Love and Peace' and superseding the line:

'Yours sincerely'.

However, since this is a letter from a very close friend, his ending seems very much more appropriate than the headings of the beginning of the letter.

One interesting feature is the way in which each letter is allocated a catch phrase. Her list of contents is put down in a way which not only points out the theme of each letter and indicates the kinds of groupings she sees in the material, but also adds a freshness to the whole which makes it more entertaining to read:

1. The 'Business-like' Tone
2. '...the gossip about life in sunny B'ham...'
3. 'Please excuse the paper.'
4. 'Keep in touch.'
5. '...better late than never.'

and so on.

Her commentary on the first letter shows very clearly the pattern of development she follows in her observations. First she describes the relationship between writer and reader and then goes on to show how this is realized through the graphics, grammar and vocabulary where appropriate, as well as in the way it is reflected in the general structure of the letter. Finally, she comments on how the letter fits into the normal conventions of letter-writing. Of course, there are many more things she could have said and some she could have expressed better; but on the whole this aspect of her project is carried out well for someone who has had a bare minimum of practice in looking at language.

Her conclusions are introduced in a purposeful and interesting way:

'This study of letters, their language, the contents as suggested by the language and the whole tone of the letters, created as a result of the various types of language used, have all been studied on the basis of my own observations.

The language used in letters between friends seems to have been influenced, as the study shows, by the nature of the relationship between writer and recipient. By this I mean whether in fact they share mutual social activities or not or whether they have associated together in the same social clique or have lived very closely together. The language also seems to vary between each writer, in each letter, because of the very fact that all writers are individuals, interpreting and making use of a device which is culturally influenced, i.e. speech and its transposition into writing. Finally, language seems to be influenced because of the very situation and idea that must be conveyed to the recipient. For example it was noted in the first letter how the writer wished to ask an important favour of a friend. He went straight to the point in a concise way. Whereas in the general conversational letter (letter 7) the writer was only concerned to discuss the news of examination results and various other miscellaneous topics.

She then takes up and discusses such features as personality, content, register, sex, correctness and purpose of writing, all her comments being based at a general level on observations she has already made in her commentary, and ends on this climactic note:

These observations in this study do not set out to prove any theories or hypotheses. They do however try to make anyone who reads them (and this has also been my experience making this study) more aware of the great diversity in style and presentation of letters written between friends. This in turn, by demonstrating how diverse language can be between individuals (besides being the common denominator for all communication) shows very startlingly and visibly that outside the range of this small, microscopic study, a whole universe of language and many other types of letter exist. Besides this immense diversity, the study has also illustrated the clichés and conventions repeatedly used and the very similar topics of discussion. But in all this, whether one observes similarity in each letter, or individuality, one cannot fail to observe that no human being who communicates using written language, is an automaton in the way he uses it—he is like the artist—he creates a work of art that reflects his own colourful or dull interior, that reflects his own opinions, that reflects himself.

Posters and Headlines

Both previous studies concerned themselves with extended prose. We now turn to two projects which look at a very different area of the written mode. This involves an examination of two forms of language which, while having a great deal in common linguistically, yet differ significantly in context. The projects illustrate also the different kinds of focus a student may choose.

The first of these is entitled *The Language of Posters*. What is original about this study is that the student not only collected her text from a well-defined area, in this case the Bullring in Birmingham, but also interviewed passers-by about their reaction to posters in general. Perhaps she could have extended this by referring them more specifically to the posters in view; but nevertheless it gave her a novel starting point for her project and enabled her to draw certain general conclusions about people's attitudes to the language medium she has chosen.

The questions she asked were:

1. Do you notice posters?
2. What draws your attention to them?
3. Do you ever notice the words on posters? Why?
4. Do you ever read posters?
5. Is there any type of poster that you do not like and think ought to be banned?
6. Is there any type of poster that particularly attracts your attention, or any poster you remember well?

The response she got was entertaining and informative. Thus she writes:

People seem to remember amusing posters more. Two ladies recalled the Andrew's Liver Salts poster of the 1920s, showing a rotund gentleman scratching his head and looking into his case, his back to the audience and a tin of Andrew's in his back pocket, saying:

'I must have left it behind.'

While a number of people remembered, but disliked, W. Little's poster of 1946, of the 'Black Widow', a poster against careless driving, although it was the appearance of the widow, not the wording, that caused offence.

98

From the general response to her questions, she concludes her introduction with:

People's reaction to posters is very important in designing them. To be successful, a poster must accomplish several things:
  1. Attract the attention of the audience.
  2. Retain the attention once attracted.
  3. It must be remembered, or at any rate recognised as familiar.
  4. It must prompt the right reaction.
Considering these points, a poster like the Andrew's advert must have been very successful. A poster does not usually rely totally on the design and pictorial effect; a considerable emphasis is placed on the words—the words themselves, how they are used, and how they are presented.

She then goes on to discuss the effectiveness of the posters she saw within a hundred yards or so of the place she held her interviews, first however giving a general description of the language features she thought she was likely to find in them:

It may be considered that the language of posters comes under the heading 'loaded language', but a slightly different language from that of television commercials or political propaganda. Poster language has a very precise, material goal, besides the fact that there is a limited writing space.
  The language has to be concise and to the point; advertisers and propagandists in other fields tend to use abstractions more.

In this project the text itself is not presented as a block at the beginning of the study, but various advertisements are quoted as they are used to illustrate a point. Thus:

COME AND SEE US SOMETIME (British Midland Airways)
DEAD ROOM; LIVING FIRE; LIVING ROOM (Coal Board)
HAD ANY YO-HO-HO LATELY (Captain Morgan's Rum)

are all used to illustrate the difference between 'direct and indirect address'. A more delicate treatment would then relate this to the grammatical categories of person and mood; but we feel reasonably satisfied when a student shows sufficient perception to indicate that he is aware that there are categories of difference.

Other groupings of this sort are:

GUARANTEED EXCELLENCE (Player's No 6)
GUARANTEED QUALITY (Player's No 10)
THE BEST TOBACCO MONEY CAN BUY (Rothman's King Size)

in which we find put together the semantic category she terms 'loaded' and the situational feature 'cigarettes'. It would not be fair to expect a student being introduced to language study in this way to be able to discriminate very finely between linguistic categories or to use a more precise terminology; but it is encouraging that the very act of studying language in this way makes the student herself set the ground, as it were, for more advanced work.

We can end our look at this project with a last quotation in which the student observes the use of what may loosely be called rhetorical devices:

The play on words is continually used in posters:
'YOU CAN BANK ON THE FUTURE...
WITH THE BIRMINGHAM MUNICIPAL BANK'
There is a use of the comedy element also, something which has been retained throughout the history of posters in Britain. This is seen in a poster for Anchor dairy products:
'WE GOT CHEESED OFF...
JUST MAKING BRITAIN'S FAVOURITE BUTTER'
This also says considerably more than the fact that Anchor now make cheese—that their butter is the 'favourite' in Britain.'

If the categorization employed seems rather unstructured, yet the possibility for further development is very clear in this study. What is more encouraging is that this student has begun to realize to what extent language impinges upon us every moment of the day, in areas that perhaps formerly she would not have considered open to objective observation.

Very similar to the last project is one on *Newspaper Headlines*. The focus here is quite different, yet it arises from the same kind of situation—utilizing material immediately available in an everyday situation. Here the student describes where she got the impetus for choosing this area of study:

'I chose the subject of newspaper headlines for my study through working in a newsagent's shop at the weekends, where I became aware of the wide range of daily newspapers available and their readership in the particular community. What was immediately noticeable was that each paper had an appeal to a different set of people. What interested me was whether a certain 'type' of person was likely to prefer a particular newspaper, and if so, why.

I therefore decided to look at the papers to see how they differed even when they all covered the same main items of the day. It was at once apparent that the headlines played a key part in the appeal of newspapers. They arrested the attention and I was able to make guesses of what kind of readership they expected or wanted, and so worded their headlines accordingly. These headlines were, of course, relying on consumer reaction, so that whilst giving the relevant information they also had to promote interest and curiosity.

This student, even more than the previous one, attempts a formally structured approach. First she decided to take three headlines from *The Times*, the *Daily Express* and the *Sun* of 21st October, 1972 as her main text for analysis, and to support her conclusions with other headlines taken from the same copies of these editions.

The text, therefore, is extremely limited:

The Times	MPs vote for jury service at 18
Express	Boys (AND GIRLS) of the jury...
Sun	TRIAL BY TEENAGER

To this text she decided to apply the following categories:

1. Size of letters in headline and space allocation
2. Placing—(a) in the paper as a whole
           (b) on the actual page
3. Actual wording of headline
           (a) familiarity of saying
           (b) play on words—puns

(c) (supposed) words of speaker
(d) exaggeration for effect (hyperbole)

She then deals with each headline in turn. The following is one of these commentaries:

The *Express* immediately became evident as a 'middle' paper—not as staid as *The Times* nor as extrovert as the *Sun*. Surprisingly, the jury service issue was not placed on the front page even, let alone as the main headline. Instead, it was placed at the bottom left of page 17 (total of 24 pages). However, it did display a restricted use of serif on seven of the thirteen larger letters and in fact all of the small capitals in brackets. It also displayed certain similar techniques included in the *Sun*, that is the use of word association. Its main letters formed 'Boys of the jury...' a deliberate ploy to suggest the phrase 'Gentlemen of the jury—' in our minds. (Incidentally this gives some indication of the expected readership, as one would expect a middle class reader to be more familiar with legal jargon than a member of the working class.) However, the addition of 'AND GIRLS' in brackets was necessary so as not to mislead the reader into thinking that only eighteen-year-old males were to be considered for jury service, and yet this was presented sufficiently small so as not to detract from the impact of the headline. However, this headline cannot be likened to that of the *Sun* to attract a 'floating' reader as it was not even on the front page. One supposes it was intended to sustain interest throughout. One also supposes or presumes that like *The Times* the *Express* is catering for its 'won' readership.

It would, of course, be possible to criticize this on a number of counts; we were nevertheless quite impressed by the amount of information this student was able to get from her text and the extent to which, in using her 'intuition', she prepared the ground for further expansion and clarification in a more structured manner at a later date.

The supportive material this student uses and comments on is not put together so promisingly, consisting for the most part of a set of unordered 'footnotes' on a random selection of headlines from the same newspapers. But she does draw these together with the more sustained examination of her main text to form a series of six conclusions which, though rather overgeneralized on the basis of the evidence, yet encourage one to realize that she has made

102

a good start towards understanding the need for close observation and the making of hypotheses.

Two of these conclusions are:

1. The *Sun* caters for the 'floating' reader who will buy because his interest and curiosity are aroused.
   The Times has a set readership and gives them what they want.
   The *Express* has a set readership and caters for them, and yet wants to attract new readers also.
2. The *Sun*'s keyword is SENSATIONALISM.
   The Times sticks to facts.
   The *Express* sticks to facts.

It is worth making a final comment of this project. In her examination of the *Sun* headline, she makes the comment:

This idea of word association is very important one, especially in this particular title, because the two words have no relevance to each other. Words have certain families:
TRIAL jury, *court*, magistrate, judge, solemnity, etc.
TEENAGER youth, *delinquency*, frivolity, foolishness, etc.
In fact, the two words underlined have a connection, but rather an unsavoury one!

It is interesting how, by playing this simple 'association' game, she draws near, quite unprompted, to an understanding not only of the notions of semantic field and collocation, but also of one of the more popular rhetorical tricks used in the language of headlines.

Film Reviews

Our final example of project work done in connection with written language is a study of *Film Reviews*. In many ways this is a typical focus used in the study of written language. As in the project on *Letters* the text is a series of short passages of continuous prose; but, where *Letters* tended to look more to the relationship between producer and audience, this study adds the further dimension of

103

the constraints imposed upon the writer by the content or subject matter of the writing. To some extent, then, this is a study in the wide area of *register* already discussed in Chapter 3.

It is important in this kind of study to make sure that the text is not too long, and in this case it was an important criterion used in the selection of the text. Essentially it meant choosing a range of reviews upon a single film. At the time of writing the film *A Clockwork Orange* was getting a great deal of attention in the press, and so was chosen as being likely to be reviewed by a wider range of magazines and newspapers than average. In fact the student managed to obtain reviews from twelve sources: *New Statesman, Evening Standard, The Times, Sunday Times, The Guardian, Time Out, Daily Mail, Morning Star, Punch, Daily Mirror, Sunday Express, The People.* It can be imagined that this alone involved the student in some useful research activity in connection with libraries and the public relations department of newspapers.

The basis of the project is a detailed examination of these reviews in turn, the length of observations being roughly proportionate to the length of each review. Before doing this, however, she presents, in table form, certain measurable features from all the texts. First we have a breakdown by number of words, sentences and paragraphs, followed by an attempt to put these together in a sort of 'order of complexity' to establish certain hypotheses about reader expectation. The value of doing this is, of course, debatable, especially with a short text. But we find that students on the whole get a lot of impetus from carrying out an activity they can fairly easily perform. Questions of validity and justification can come later. But it is quite remarkable how consistently journals with fewer words per sentence will also have shorter paragraphs in number of sentences per paragraph; and students like to find this out for themselves. Another measurement made in this project is the amount of space given in each review to story line, acting and music, and the space given in each journal to reviews and the arts in general. This set of measurements, of course, will broadly fit in with the first set. Again, this may be a questionable activity in some ways, since all sorts of questions may be asked about the units of measurements. But it does bring to light certain problems of methodology, and makes students ask basic questions about establishing criteria for measurement and about the value of statistics in language analysis.

Quite accidentally the student, in picking this film, chose one in which language itself is used in a unique way. He uses this as an addendum and draws together all comments from the reviews in which this fact was mentioned:

New Statesman over-rich argot drawing heavily on Russian transliterations.
Evening Standard callous slang vocabulary with Russian roots.
The Times Russianized English argot.
Sunday Times teenagers' slang, James Joyce, only much easier.
The Guardian Cockney-Romany-Russian argot.
Time Out a primitive composite of Cockney and Slavonic.
Daily Mail a language largely his own peppered with words like....
Morning Star curious jargon he speaks in, Lennon English, peppered with Russki Russianisms.
Daily Mirror they talk in a groovy, poetic slang.

Unfortunately, he leaves it at that, not realizing what a rich text he already has, worth in fact a project on its own. Two comments, however, would have been worth making: (a) on the attitudes towards language on the part of the reviewers; and (b) the difficulties of a writer trying to convey information to readers who might never have seen the film nor read the book on which it was based. There is also the suggestion, incidentally, that some of the reviewers didn't know what was going on themselves.

The rest of the study is taken up with the commentaries on individual texts. The largest of these are too long to quote, but we present here two of the shorter ones:

The Times contains the third largest review and according to the statistics gives about $7\frac{1}{2}\%$ arts coverage.

Only 12% is given to relating the story but a huge 36% is given to discussing the actors and quality of acting. This may reveal how the writer judges his audience's cultural attitude to drama as a whole. One might presume from this that *Times* readers are expected to be keen theatre goers and particularly interested in this aspect of the cinema. Since he is concerned with the visual aspects and quality of photography, appropriate to the subject, he refers to and comments on John Alcott—the cameraman.

Music gets about 6% coverage: Rossini and Purcell are named. Beethoven is referred to as
'Ludwig von'
and this implies an expected level of audience knowledge.

He refers to Nadsat as 'Russianized English argot'.

The reviewer himself is confident his audience will understand the word argot. The nearest he comes himself to this style of language is 'rape-cum-beating-up'. Whereas most other reviewers refer to Anthony Burgess's novel in passing, this one discusses the postulations of the novel before attempting to discuss Kubrick's interpretation of it.

He expects an all-round cultural interest by his audience. He is quite cool in his approach. This is shown in his use of the non-committal 'hero' as a description of Alex. He does not use emotive terms to bias his audience's estimation of Alex. He seems to have a high opinion of his audience, and has no wish to spoon-feed them. He assumes a rudimentary knowledge of Kubrick's past films and McDowell's film 'If', and also a film involving another actor.

The reviewer uses phrases like rape-cum-beating-up to avoid using a conventional emotive word and wanting to describe the scene with lurid details. He uses the word violence 3 times and considering the subject of the film this is difficult.

Within the title of his review he opts for the clockwork part of the orange and chooses

'Brilliant intricate mechanism of the Clockwork Orange.' He also criticizes a sentence in similar vein:

'The whole thing works with, yes, the absolute precision of clockwork.'

This phrase surprised me, coming from the *Times*. It seemed rather a weak concoction.

Structurally the *Times* review has the largest sentences and long paragraphs. The vocabulary is not difficult; only words like divagate and argot might pose problems. It is far less complex in this respect than *Time Out*. The language is less colourful and popular than that of the *Standard*. There are obvious expectations of an educated, cultured audience with interests in other fields. His 'low-profile' approach implies he is communicating with a reasonably intellectual audience, not a conservative or right-wing audience who might expect a more reactionary approach.

Sunday Express gives the highest percentage to story telling—75%. Interestingly though 95% of this deals with the story of the film after Alex's arrest. The writer obviously does not wish to exploit the violence in the film as the Mail did.

This is how he describes what took the Mail 95% to say:

'Set in the near future, it is about a young lad called Alex who takes delight in smashing everyone and everything in reach, on whim.'

He raises the moral questions.

There are very little audience expectations. He does not presume a particular attitude. The sentences are short and so are the paragraphs; there are no difficult words.

It is at this point that we come back to a difficulty mentioned earlier in the chapter, that the students have so well learned the habit of placing emphasis on their response to a piece of writing, and, incidentally, giving little importance to matters of punctuation and style, that it takes some time for them to focus a less personal eye on the text before them. This comes through quite clearly in these passages. Thus we find the *Times* writer is 'quite cool in his approach' and the term *hero* is described as 'non-committal'; elsewhere sentences are characterized as of 'reasonable' length and vocabulary as 'pseudo-intellectual'. To be fair to this student, however, he does this rather less frequently than average.

What must, however, be said on the positive side about all these projects on written language is that, in the very area where they are most likely to find it difficult to throw off the yoke of A-level writing (remember that they are all 'English' students), we find a clear and determined attempt to discover what are the data on which comment might be made, and how to relate sentence length or features of audience or context to the wider meaning of a text. This is quite encouraging, however faltering and inadequate it may seem. It is even more rewarding to see the growing awareness of students that they are dealing with a complex linguistic situation which, for all its complexity, yet can be discovered, by their own efforts, to certain fundamental and ultimately describable dimensions—grammar, audience, context, and so on—which can be used to draw meaning out of a text in ways they had not thought possible before.

It may be worth repeating at this point what is the underlying assumption of all work of this kind: that it is for the teacher to devise strategies to enable the learner to make explicit what is already within himself, the ability to use language efficiently. What we find also is that success, however minimal, on the part of the student in externalizing and objectifying what in some sense he already knows is one of the most rewarding aspects of doing a language project for both teacher and taught alike.

6 Problems and procedures

Previous chapters have been concerned with a number of individual projects selected from a number of language areas. The present chapter tries to generalize about some of these difficulties encountered by students in making their choices, and by tutors in guiding them to make that choice and in helping them to develop techniques which can enable them to describe their chosen text. To put it another way, whereas up to now we have concentrated on work already done, by us and our own students, we now go on to make suggestions for similar work to be done by others.

The focus of our attention will therefore be on the kinds of problem that teacher and students will be likely to meet in setting out to study a particular area of language, and on the procedures that we have found useful in overcoming some of these problems. We are not suggesting that we have found all the answers. We are not even supposing that we have discovered all the questions. But we suspect that a teacher who does a series of projects with a group of students is likely to meet the same sorts of difficulties we did. We therefore offer our own experience more as an encouragement than a guide.

Student or Teacher Choice

When a student is asked to initiate a language project, the teacher has two options open to him. He can either impose a topic on the student or allow him to choose his own. If the former course is taken, many of the problems discussed here become minimal— or rather they become problems for the teacher instead of the student. We ourselves have always allowed the student to choose, on the grounds that it is likely to lead to greater commitment if he is investigating language he has discovered for himself. We have no real evidence to support this claim. But on those few occasions when a student has completely failed to find a text, so that we have given him a 'second-hand' one for him to describe, the results have tended to be disappointing. We are not suggesting by this that all the other students are not also being in some sense guided by us in certain directions. More often it happens that a student is guided away from certain topics whose intrinsic difficulty they are not aware of. But on the whole we try to leave the burden of choice with the student.

This approach, however, immediately confronts him with difficulties of four kinds: selection of topic; collection of material; analysis of the material; and presentation of the study. The rest of this chapter will be devoted to an examination of these areas. It must be borne in mind, of course, that we are talking specifically about the kinds of students described in Chapter 1. We feel, however, that our comments are equally applicable to other kinds of students in other types of institution.

Doing a Language Project

Selecting a topic
In many ways this is the most perplexing aspect of doing project work as far as the student is concerned. What happens, at least in most cases, is that a student will eventually settle on some area that he is able to investigate with profit; but only after a period of uncertainty during which he picks up and discards a variety of topics before arriving at the one which, for him, is both feasible and interesting.

The initial difficulty stems from a sense of his own inadequacy in a completely new discipline, combined with the overwhelming number of language 'events' from which he may select a text. It is indeed more complicated than this, since many students will choose an area in the hope that they will be able to collect a text which does not yet exist, only to find that their hopes are illusory. This is especially the case in spoken language. The only way out of this dilemma, short of the teacher allocating topics to individual students, is for both teacher and pupil to exercise restraint and patience. We're not sure how to get students to do this! But in allowing two terms for a project from introduction to completion, we are reasonably satisfied if the student has made his selection by the middle of the first term. Many students take longer than this. Some have even made an initial choice and started work on it by the end of the first term only to change their minds and begin a new topic at the beginning of the second. These are the exceptions, however, and the fact that they often succeed in turning in an acceptable piece of work does not mean that the average student is capable of this. One of the reasons why this change of mind occurs is that students on the whole tend to underestimate the difficulty of collecting their data. We shall return to this in the next section.

There are two kinds of problems associated with selecting a topic. The first of these is related to the initial introduction of the concept of language project work; the second to the follow up period, when students are trying to narrow their attention to a particular area of study.

How the first introduction is made will largely depend on the number of students involved. In our case we have had to introduce the general idea to as many as one hundred students in any one year. The most effective way to do this seems to be a short lecture, followed by meeting students in small groups of between a dozen and twenty in order to discuss in greater detail the kinds of problems introduced in the lecture. Eventually the numbers in the groups are reduced still further until, once the projects have got under way, the basis of teacher–student contact is the tutorial group, involving one or two students at each meeting, or at most three.

We have discovered through experience that the initial lecture should be both short, perhaps half an hour, and simple. On one occasion we tried to support the lecture by distributing a fairly comprehensive hand-out containing about seventy possible areas of study together with suggestions of how the different areas could be tackled. In the event this was a failure, since the students were overwhelmed by the seeming complexity of the task at the very start and were daunted before they began.

What we do now is simply to convey to the students a message which, at risk of oversimplification, is something like this: 'For almost all your waking hours you are bombarded by language in one form or another. What we want you to do is to use your eyes and your ears to select from that huge babel of messages any aspect of language you would like to study in detail.' To help with this we give each student a simple hand-out delineating the main theme of the lecture. (A copy of this is appended at the end of the chapter.)

At this point the student is left to mull over the general nature of the task for a few days before we start to familiarize him, in seminar groups, with the kinds of problems he is likely to face in making his choice. He is then asked to nominate about three topics so that he can see the kinds of problems each presents. In this way he is better able to settle on the one most likely to be suitable for his own circumstances.

If, in presenting these problems to the reader, we are forced to separate them, we must remind him that they are not so easily separable in practice. We suggest that these problems of selection involve decisions about: delineating the area to be studied; making assumptions about collecting a text in that area; and trying to determine what non-linguistic data needs to be collected if the analysis of the text is to be meaningful.

Delineating an area of choice

The main problem here is really one of scale. A student's first re-action is to want to study an 'area' rather than a 'text'. Thus a common choice is: 'Yorkshire Dialect' or 'Posters' or 'Poetry'. There is often a whiff of ardour about the way they respond at this level, and it is sometimes difficult to point out that they are not being asked to write a book. It could be argued, of course, that they should be allowed to find out the impossibility of the task they have set themselves through experience. But we have found that when students persist in this generalized approach they almost invariably end up discouraged and usually turn in a piece of work that is below average.

The task of the teacher is to turn the mind of the student to a different order of question. If we relate it to the three suggestions above, they might be: 'I've got a great aunt who speaks broad Yorkshire. I'd like to get a tape of her and study that'; or 'There's a building development down the road and the fencing around it is plastered with adverts and notices. How would I set about looking at the language on them?'; or simply (though often disastrously) 'What about comparing two pop songs?' The point, then, is that not only does a short text enable the student to have more clearly defined boundaries, it also shows him that a very small, perhaps apparently trivial, area of language can provide an adequate text for a very deep study. The last chapter is a good example of this.

We think that the main point at issue here has been made, but one other of some importance remains. This is the linguistic focus, which needs to be considered even as early as this, since it can have a profound influence on the ultimate result. By this we mean whether the analysis is going to be in the direction of features predominantly phonological, grammatical and lexical or semantic, or some combination of some or all of these. For example, a student could spend a lot of time transcribing the tape of his Yorkshire aunt, and using inadequate phonetic symbols to do so, when his main interest was in trying to relate her vocabulary to the history and geography of the village in which she was born. Alternatively, if his main interest was in the sounds she made, he could more profitably spend much of the time he would use in trying to collect and transcribe a long tape in learning something about phonetics.

Feasibility of getting a text

Some students are born optimists. Some of them are also born innocents. We give two examples of each kind.

The optimists. A number of students are taken with the idea of looking at the language of gravestones. The gothic romance of the notion soon palls however after a few cold, wet mornings discovering that, for the most part, one gravestone is very much like another. One student soon came to the conclusion that there was little to be gained by this activity until she wondered whether the language on a gravestone might be constrained by the hardness of the stone used by the mason and whether this in turn was conditioned by the geology of the region. In the event she did a very good piece of work. But we are not quite sure if what she did was an exercise in language or stone-rubbing.

Another optimist wished to find out about the language of street-traders. Again, the result was quite pleasing, in that he learnt a lot from what he did. But we suspect that his main lesson was that it is not as easy as it seems to sell apples, and that it is even more difficult to make a good tape-recording on a busy street.

The innocents. One student had the bright idea of trying to find out what linguistic changes occur in a speaker under the influence of alcohol. His intention was to tape-record his girl-friend when sober and then to get her drunk, when he would make another recording. He never quite managed to see why we objected to this way of conducting a language project.

Perhaps the most innocent of all our students was one who was determined to study the language of a local group of Hell's Angels. For about six weeks he regularly attended the pub where they met and gradually became acquainted with them. In the course of doing this he had his overcoat stolen and got himself beaten up. It is not difficult to imagine his chagrin when, at the end of his travail, they refused to let him tape them. We eventually suggested that he study language development in a group of five year olds.

There are many constraints that can operate against the collection of an adequate text for study. Some of them will be unforeseen; some can to some extent be anticipated. But in essence all the teacher can do is to caution the student against the more obvious ones and to stress that he should try to have some advance knowledge, from the very beginning, of which direction his project is likely to go. This may be particularly the case where a comparative study is being made. A student may, for example, decide to study the way the language of advertisements changes through different magazines or through a long run of the same magazine. They often do this because they just happen to have a few of their potential texts at hand. It is sometimes difficult for them to see that it may not be all that easy to obtain the material necessary to fill the gaps.

Availability of the non-textual data
One of the things we try constantly to impress upon the students is that they must place the text they are using in its appropriate context. One of the dangers of this is that some students pay much more attention to the situational than to the linguistic features. On the whole, however, this is often more acceptable than the work of the occasional student who goes too far in the opposite direction. An example of the latter is the student who decided to study the language of Christmas cards and who found herself with such stereotyped data that she could do little else than compile rather tedious lists of lexical and grammatical patterns. The problem was essentially one of selection, since if she had taken a different focus at the beginning and widened her scope to include historical evidence she might have ended up with a more interesting study. At the same time, if she had done so, she might well have discovered difficulties in obtaining suitable texts from the past. No doubt this could have been overcome in turn by consulting secondary evidence, since diligent research would no doubt come across books and magazine articles on the history of greetings cards. But generally we try to discourage this kind of work, preferring students to use first-hand texts wherever possible.

It is one of the most important tasks of the teacher to bring about a balance among all these possibilities, and we cannot stress enough that a careful consideration of difficulties at the time of the selection of topic can save a great deal of trouble later on. Above all, care needs to be taken in deciding the focus of the study, since this will determine the kind of supportive data that needs to be collected, wherever possible simultaneously with the text. A few examples might serve to make the point.

A not uncommon area of choice among students is that of language development in children. One student decided to study the linguistic changes that occurred over a period of about four months in her baby sister, who was just over three years old. Since she was interested in general development, it was fortunate that in making her tapes she was careful to note down the non-linguistic features such as gestures and objects in the room at the same time. Without these she might have been forced to narrow her aim to phonological or grammatical changes only, and this was not her intention.

Another popular area is that of women's magazines. A common focus here is on the class bias that seems to occur over the range. There is of course the whole problem of defining the notion of class involved in this, and most students are not really aware of how difficult this is. A more particular problem is connected with finding out the expectation of magazine editors. A number of our students have tried to get data of this area by writing to the various magazines they are interested in, but with little success. Not that they do not get replies, but that the replies are at best evasive. The same thing tends to occur with any project connected with the mass media, and perhaps it is understandable that it should be so. But it is difficult to convince students that the data they want is so difficult to obtain. By the time they have found out for themselves it is often too late to change the direction of their project and they have to make do with inadequate supportive data.

It is impossible to be precise on the theme of selection of topic. Each choice generates its own problems, though often this in itself acts as a stimulus to students. The teacher must be aware, however, that problems of collection and analysis must somehow be anticipated during the whole period given to initial selection if the student is to avoid frustration and eventual apathy.

Collecting the data
We have already discussed some of the problems involved in collecting data in our previous section. We shall now assume that the student has made his choice of topic and consider the more specific difficulties which may arise at this point. Our emphasis here then it not so much on what data to collect, but how it is collected. Since there are two kinds of data, linguistic and non-linguistic, it will be convenient to discuss these separately.

The collection of the textual data will have two quite different kinds of problems depending on whether the text is written or spoken. In both these cases, however, the same kinds of problems occur in topics where the text is potential rather than actual.

Where the text already exists, the only question that arises is to find out where it is. Often this is no problem at all, since many students select their topics on the basis that they already have a text available. Literary projects are an example of this, though these may well be discouraged since they are not the easiest to analyse. Many families have records of some sort or another, ranging from tapes of young children to old school exercise books or bundles of letters. Public libraries are obvious sources of texts, as are those associated with various institutions such as newspapers. Many of these will provide photostat copies of what they have on file. But many difficulties can occur. For instance, one student wished to trace the historical and geographical variants of a particular folk song, a simple idea in principle which in practice turned out to be very complicated. She was aware that the texts she wanted were in existence somewhere, but actually to trace more than five or six in the time available proved impossible. In this whole area luck is a very large component; the other is perseverance.

When it comes to using texts that are as yet in the future, there is almost an element of gambling involved. In the case of children's language development, for example, it is difficult to forecast that a tape can be obtained which will exhibit features that, for students of little linguistic sophistication, will be comparable to other tapes. One way out of this, of course, is to set up test conditions which will elicit the features being looked for; but this brings about problems of procedures and methodology rather beyond the kind of task we try to set our students. Sometimes, too, one must be prepared to wait until a text emerges. A simple case of this is the student who decided to compare the different ways newspapers handle the news. In order to do this he wished to find a day when at least two important items of news would be reported in all newspapers to which he had access. All he had to do was wait and look. But he could have waited a long time.

Where speech is concerned special problems of a technical nature occur. Most students do not realize how difficult it is to obtain a good, workable spoken text. They underestimate too the length of time it takes to make an acceptable transcription, and rarely consider in advance how precise their transcription needs to be or which non-linguistic features must be included. Because many of the most interesting topics are associated with casual, everyday situations—children playing, women gossiping in a supermarket, a bus conductor 'chatting up a bird'—they tend to go for such topics without realizing what they might be letting themselves in for.

The collection of data intended to support and elucidate the text is something that must be thought about as early as possible. Often the collection of this secondary data is easier than the primary, linguistic text. In some ways it is also more interesting for the average student to describe, for example, what sort of a person Jeremiah Bloggs is than to focus on what he is saying or writing. An over-zealous collection of secondary data can distort the whole study simply because the student, having amassed it, is determined to use it. A good example of this is the student who wished to study a dialect play. He already had a collection of texts to choose from and, in the course of working on them, became acquainted with the author. At this point the direction of his study changed, since the author was much more interesting—though not linguistically—than the plays.

Another important aspect of the collection of secondary data is deciding which kind is the most relevant to the focus of the study. A common interest among our students is in the attitudes that people have towards language. The text in this case too often becomes merely the starting point for another kind of study, either sociological or occasionally psychological. Associated with this tends to be the use of questionnaires, which seem academically fashionable to certain students. The trouble with this is, once again, the change of focus; but at the same time students have little awareness of how hard it is to devise and operate questionnaires in a meaningful way. On the other hand, this desire might be used to initiate a joint study with some other department in the college.

Analysis and contextualization

Once the student has made his selection of topic and collected the necessary text and supportive data, he has two tasks facing him before he gets to the stage of writing out his study in an acceptable form. The first of these is to analyse his text to determine which linguistic features are significant for the focus he has in mind. The second is to match these features against the non-linguistic data he has collected. These two processes will tend to occur simultaneously in most cases. Putting it another way, his text will reveal what is said or written; his analysis will show how it was put together; and the matching of analysis with supportive data, which we call contextualization, will answer questions relating to who spoke or wrote the text on what occasion and for what purpose.

It is now, more than at any other time, that a student needs tutorial guidance. We view the task of the teacher as being sixfold:

1. To determine the level of competence the student already has, in particular his ability to notice and to describe with reasonable objectivity the linguistic features which are important. As we suggested in Chapter One, a teacher would be wise to make few assumptions about this.

2. To channel the student into making a description appropriate to his particular area, using, where possible, those terms with which the student is already familiar and correcting them where necessary; but always ready to encourage the student to develop his own terminology. Students in general fight shy of using linguistic terms; they are even more reluctant to experiment with their own. We feel one of the most useful aspects of a language project can be that students who have completed one are no longer so lacking in confidence in this area.

3. To explore with the student the notion of delicacy, that is the degree of finesse in description which is appropriate to the focus the student wishes to make. The area of study where it is easiest to see the importance of this is perhaps in the description of sounds. So many students wish to describe, for example, a dialect text without any realization of the extent to which they must first become acquainted with phonetic and phonological principles. That it is perhaps even more difficult at the levels of grammar and semantics is not so easy to see.

4. To offer a continuous feedback situation in which students are encouraged to believe in their capacities for making analyses (and it is as easy to underestimate students in this respect as it

is to overestimate them); and in which students are weaned gently away from the preconceptions about language which they bring with them, especially where attitudes towards correctness are concerned.

These four guidelines are mainly concerned with the student's analysis of the text. The next two are more to do with contextualization and relate to the teacher.

5. To determine with the student what is relevant in the text to what he knows about the context. This is obviously associated with the notion of *focus* which we have already used a number of times. But there is also the question of how far certain features are 'easy' or 'obvious', so that, without sufficient care, they become overstressed. Some examples may help. Some students may hit upon the notion that it is easy to measure sentence length, say in comics, by counting words without first coming to terms with the fact that their notions about *word* or *sentence* need to be evaluated; and, quite as important, without asking themselves whether they have any meaningful way of relating sentence length to the context they are studying, which in this case includes not just the comic itself but also the potential reader. In the same way students looking at bias in newspapers get too involved in measuring the size of type and fail to notice that the syntactic features of their text are much more relevant to their purpose. A last example would be the student whose project on dialect ends up by being little more than an amorphous word list, often of plants and animals.

6. To help the student draw together the various threads of investigation he has followed so that the final result will be coherent and satisfying. A language project ideally will set the scene in which a text occurs, and then relate specific features in that scene to those in the text. To achieve a balance between these two comes only out of a teacher-student partnership. (We would like to stress that we are talking about the 'ideal' situation—we do not claim ever to have been in it!) A measure of the success of the partnership can usually be found in the degree of coherence and balance present in the final presentation of the study.

Presentation
One of the most recurrent themes of student discussion when they begin to do a language project is: what shape will it have? Closely connected to this is another obsession: how many words will be

necessary? The difficulty usually arises with those students whose main experience with writing has been 'doing essays'. It is only fair to say that most students quickly get over this initial uncertainty. There remain a few, however, who never get rid of the notion that any respectable work must take the shape of an essay. So deeply entrenched is this with a handful of them that it conditions not just their approach but even their initial selection. These are the students who tend to choose 'The Language of Poetry' or 'Language and Philosophy' or 'Advertising: why does it misuse language?' What can be done with this small but persistent hard core of students it is hard to say. The problem would seem at first sight to be solvable in a one to one tutorial situation. But we do not find this to be the case. Often, in fact, these students take more tutorial time than any others and yet never budge from their initial prejudice.

Most students, however, soon acclimatize themselves to realize that each topic will generate its own structure, and that length need not be counted only in words. Once they have experimented with trying to make an adequate tape-recording and transcribing it, or analysing the structure of a piece of children's writing, or devising a perceptive questionnaire, they soon accept that 'work' is not just reading books and writing essays, and they usually come to enjoy this different kind of activity.

At the same time we try to offer them a framework on which they can hang their final presentation, stressing all the time that it is suitable for only some kinds of study and that no-one should tailor his study to suit this framework. We suggest also that we do not object to headings and sub-headings, nor to a 'personalized' approach provided that the terminology is acceptable.

In offering this framework to the reader we do so with the realization that it is not only inappropriate to certain kinds of study, but may also be inappropriate for some kinds of students. We offer it simply because we have found it useful as a starting point for discussion about the question of presentation. The framework we suggest is this:

A   Background
  1. why the student chose to do *this* study and the kind of focus being used;
  2. method of collecting data and difficulties encountered;
  3. description of relevant supportive data: the people involved, features in the situation, publishing details of a text from a written source, etc;

4. hypothesis: what kinds of conclusions can one anticipate?
(this is sometimes better put first)
B The Text
C Analysis and Contextualization
This relates B with A3
D Conclusion, referring back to A4

We accept that the above is very much an idealized version of what we do in practice. Given the limitations of time and staffing within which we work, the procedure outlined in this chapter represents something we aim for, even if we don't always achieve it. Our intention in presenting it in this way is to indicate to teachers and lecturers who feel that they would like to try the Language Project Approach at least some of the problems they are likely to meet and to offer them some of the procedures we have tried to adopt to anticipate and overcome these problems. What must be constantly remembered, however, is that each project and each student must be dealt with in a different way. To illustrate this further, we finish, in the next chapter, by presenting in its entirety one Language Project together with a commentary relating to these problems and procedures.

English Language Project: Notes for Students

1. For this study you are being asked to take as objective a view as you can of some area where language is used. Two useful things to remember to begin with are:
   (a) that language must involve a producer and an audience;
   (b) that any language communication, however short or long, must occur in a situation of some sort.
   Your work should therefore consist of two stages:
   (a) a stage of collecting a 'text' from the area chosen;
   (b) saying something about how the 'text' is related to the producer/audience and to the situation in which the communication took place.

2. When you think of the producer/audience dimension, you may find the following useful:
   (a) idiolect: this is the language of the individual.
   (b) group-language: the language of any group of people, however small, within a linguistic community which speaks the same language, e.g. English has virtually an infinite number of varieties of group-language because the number of sub groups in the population is infinite. Each of the group-languages will show some differences from any other.
   The group can vary in size from two, e.g. a mother talking to her child, to millions, as when you compare American English with British English.
   Two particular varieties of group language you could consider are: (i) dialect and National Language, where geography is a limiting factor, and (ii) occupational group-language, the result of common interest in a job, e.g. the language of students or lawyers.

3. Besides this important dimension of language, another dimension must be considered, that of the constraint imposed upon the 'text' by the situation in which it occurs: some of the factors involved here are: (i) age of the users of the language; (ii) the physical or emotional nature of the situation (do teachers speak differently according to whether their classroom is large or small, their class disciplined or rowdy?); (iii) the social implications in the situation (are some situations more formal than others?); (iv) the degree of education or intelligence or fluency of the speakers; (v) the sex of the members of the group.

4. The suggestion is that you choose a text bearing some of these things in mind. You could find a subject from the dimension of para 2, e.g. dialect of Somerset, American English, language of legal documents or your block, with no particular reference to para 3. Or you might decide to concentrate on the dimensions of para 3, e.g. the language of lovers alone compared to their language when in company (but you must provide a tape recording to show the text is genuine and not made up!). Or you might decide to combine both sets of dimensions and describe say, the effect on the language of someone who speaks in a Yorkshire dialect when he takes a job in the South of England.

5. In describing the text itself, keep the following four areas in mind:

   (a) Sound (if you are examining speech). Consider how you would transcribe an accent to distinguish it from the pronunciation suggested in the Oxford Dictionary.

   (b) Vocabulary   { try to be consistent in your use of terminology.

   (c) Syntax

   (d) Meaning

7 The -y diminutive in the Liverpool dialect

We devote our final chapter to quoting in full the project of one student, together with comments on the sequence of steps she took in the working out of her study. In this way we hope to tie into a practical situation some of the problems and procedures we outlined in the last chapter.

When she undertook this project, the student was in her first year of teacher training, with English as her main subject. She had previously attended a grammar school and obtained A-levels in two subjects. She was therefore in many ways typical of the kind of student described in Chapter 1. For example, she was familiar with 'parts of speech' or 'syllable', but these and similar terms formed only an unorganized set of expressions that had something to do with 'language'. The notion of language itself being a coherent study was unknown to her, at least in the sense we mean.

On coming to college she came into contact with a large number of people from a wide variety of linguistic backgrounds and, as often happens, developed a vague curiosity about dialectal differences. Consequently, when she was asked in the introductory talk and subsequent tutorial to select a language area for study, she had little difficulty in selecting dialect. The particular variety she decided upon was that of her own home locality, as she explains in her introduction:

In the Autumn of 1971 I planned an essay on the Liverpool Dialect and began to collect text during the Christmas holidays. When I tried to arrange my material, I became particularly interested in the large number of words having a -y diminutive which I had collected. I had already been aware that many such words existed in the dialect, but never studied them. I therefore decided to restrict my study to this group of words, and discover if Liverpudlians follow any rules, consciously or not, when reducing or increasing words to two syllables, the second of which was -y.

I collected the text during and after the Christmas holiday, most of the examples coming from my own speech and that of my parents and a brother at school. Sometimes I began a conversation on the subject, and in this way collected more examples from friends and relatives in Liverpool.

I have used in this essay only examples which I have heard myself. None have been taken from the popular books on the subject published by Spiegl in 1966, since I wanted my study to examine the dialect as I found it between Christmas 1971 and Easter 1972. (For a brief history of the dialect see (2) pp. 10–12.)

I have however consulted the books by Spiegl, as well as Partridge's Dictionary (1), to ascertain the derivation of certain words. In Daniel Jones's book I used the notes and tables for the classification of vowels and consonants (pp. 3–26) and list of phonetic symbols (pp. xix–xxii).

The refinement of focus outlined in the first paragraph of this introduction took some time to develop. Her first impulse was to examine certain expressions, particularly euphemisms, which she found in the speech of her friends and relatives. As an example of these she quoted to us *The Birthday Cake*, a reference to Liverpool's Roman Catholic Cathedral. This, of course, is precisely that area which students do find attractive, however unpromising it really is from the point of view of a language study. No doubt she was also influenced at the beginning by the books of Fritz Spiegl which she put in her Bibliography. These were very popular at that time as part of the general interest in things Liverpudlian that was generated by the attention being paid by the media to the Mersey Sound.

Fortunately, however, she soon realized the pitfalls of vagueness and generality that could open up before her unless she defined for herself a more limiting, but coherent, text. But if it was luck that the list of expressions she had collected contained such a text, in the shape of the -y diminutives, it must be stressed that she had the percipience to recognize that, within this group of words, lay a complex patterning that it might be profitable and interesting to tease out. In doing this she found herself not only having to learn more about phonetics in general, and the phonology of Liverpudlian in particular; but she also had to come to terms with

124

the fact that, for adequate description, she needed a more precise vocabulary of grammatical terms than she already possessed. That she faced these difficulties squarely is self-evident from the use she makes of them in her study. If she also makes the occasional comment like 'the sound produced is ugly'; or an oversimplification, as when sounds are cited without reference to what are crucial features of length or stress, as in her treatment of *Adelphi* or *electricity* below, we believe that these blemishes do little to affect the overall treatment of the subject.

Let us now look at the general opening remarks of the study:

In the Liverpudlian dialect there is a tendency for certain words to become disyllabic. The new formation usually consists of a stressed syllable followed by *-y*, e.g. *cauliflower* becomes *cauly*.

Words of three or more syllables become disyllabic by a combination of their first syllable and *-y*: *cardy > cardigan*; *uny > university*; *parky > park-keeper*; *tranny > transistor*; *welly > wellington* (boot), *corpy > corporation*. Exceptions to this are formations from words whose first syllable is one of the vowel sounds. To say any of these sounds and then *-y* is very difficult and the sound produced is ugly. The second syllable is therefore used instead: *the Delly > The Adelphi Hotel*; *lecky > electricity*. Other exceptions are the words *irony* and *metally*, both of three syllables. They are the names of ball-bearings used as marbles and were formed by children, who presumably do not follow quite the same rules.

Words of two syllables remain disyllabic, but the second syllable is replaced by *-y*: *presy > present*; *milky > milkman*; *cossy > costume*; *Sefy (Park) > Sefton (Park)*; *Kirky > Kirkdale*; *sidey > sideburn*; *Chrisy > Christmas*; *docky > doctor*. An exception to this may be *sarny* for *sandwich*. In the dialect *sany* means *sanitary inspector*, so a new word for *sandwich* may have received a slight altering of the first syllable to avoid confusion. Alternatively, as the word *sarny* for *sandwich* seems widespread in areas including parts of the South of England, it may have reached Liverpool from elsewhere.

Liverpudlians enjoy the sound and music of their dialect and this may explain why even words of one syllable may become disyllabic: *Leecey Street > Leece Street*; *Marshy Laney Street > Marsh Lane Street*. (The addition of *Street* after the names of roads and lanes is not uncommon in Liverpool.)

In some cases it is difficult to know whether or not a word has developed from a monosyllable. For example, the word *cordies* may be the disyllabic form of *corduroy trousers*, or may have developed from the already shortened word *cords*, which seems to have been common in England for years. Again the word *Chinky* may have come direct from its original *Chinaman*, or have developed from *Chink*, a common usage in many parts of the country.

Another problem of derivation occurs with the word *boozery*, which means 'brewery'. This may be the Liverpudlian derivation from *boozer*, but it would be an unusual formation. More probably it comes from *booze* 'drink' with the suffix-*ery* as an alternative form to -*eria* as found in *washeteria, cafeteria*.

The example *Marshy Laney Street* above illustrates the Liverpudlian enjoyment of the sound of language. This also shows itself in a number of words in the dialect. *Finnan Haddock* is not known simply as *finny*, but *finny haddy*. Both words are given the -*y* and are linked. The compound contains the vowel sounds i-a, a common combination in English. It is found, for example, in *pitter-patter, zig-zag* and *riff-raff*. It is also found in the Liverpudlian *liblab* 'library'.

Another compound word, *conny-onny*, is used for *condensed milk*. This is the expected disyllabic form followed by nonsense rhyming syllables. A calculating female is known as a *sharpy-harpy*. According to Partridge (1), *sharpy* is a name for someone who is 'self-consciously alert'. Examples of rhyming slang are common. The words *Chrisy* 'Christmas' and *presy* 'present' were formed separately, but later linked to make *Chrisy-presy*.

The above introduces interestingly and comprehensively the scope of what she intends to do. We could have wished at this point, perhaps, for a wider discussion of the role of this particular diminutive morpheme in English, as in the very common usage of *Jackie, cabby* or even *Hello-ee*; or possibly of the function of diminutives generally. But at this stage the student prefers to get on with the examination of the data she has collected, and we do not quarrel with her for this.

The main section of the study follows. It is primarily concerned with delimiting the parts of speech affected by this usage and its relative frequency of occurrence through different word categories. Other arrangements are of course possible; but we are reasonably sure that for this student, with the extent of linguistic knowledge she had at the time she did the project, she chose the most useful organization for her material.

Almost all the words affected by this process are nouns, and there exist examples of proper nouns, count nouns (both singular and plural), mass nouns and abstract nouns.

Many proper names become disyllabic: *Charly > Charles; Kenny > Kenneth; Lenny > Leonard; Franny > Frances; Stevy > Stephen; Joey > Joseph*. Most of these, of course, are not just peculiar to the Liverpool dialect. But we also find surnames changed, particularly among boys who call each other by their surnames: *Nelly > Nelson; Morty > Mortenson; Smithy > Smith; Ducky > Duckers*. These names really belong to the language of children rather than the dialect of the region; but the forms of Christian and family names are also used from adult to adult.

Most of the proper nouns affected, however, belong to the place names of Liverpool, places that all the people living there seem to know. Many of these are street names, not all in the city centre: *Utty > Utting Avenue; Scotty > Scotland Road; Greaty > Great Homer Street; Vauxy > Vauxhall Road; Ziggy > Zigzag Road; Stranny-> Strand Road; Leecey > Leece Street; Upper Parly > Upper Parliament Street; The Bully > Princes Park Boulevard; Corny > Cornwallis Street; Wesy > Westminster Road*. The extent of this usage is shown clearly by the way an icecream shop in Westminster Road advertises its famous *Wesy Whips*.

In a few cases the words *Lane* or *Street* are kept in the new form. Exactly why Park Lane is known as *Parky Lane* I cannot be sure, unless it is both to avoid association with the more famous London version and to avoid confusion with the Liverpool term for 'park-keeper'. In the case of Smithdown Road, it has to be known as *Smithy Road* since *Smithy* is the name given to the cemetery there. The *street* in *Marshy Laney Street* is, as I have already indicated, an addition.

The names of the most frequented shops also undergo change: *Wooly's > Woolworth's; The Coey > Co-op; Marky's > Mark's and Spencer's*. Other favourite haunts are: *The Delly > The Adelphi Hotel; The Uny > The University; The Mysy > The Mystery* (an alternative name for Wavertree Park, after a past mystery regarding its ownership); *The Graffy > The Grafton (Ballroom); The Locky > The Locarno (Ballroom); The Lanny > The Landing Stage; The Casy > The Cast-iron Shore* (after the ironworks which once stood on the site).

All the above places are in Liverpool and are well-known to its inhabitants. An exception is *Newy > New Brighton*, the only place outside Liverpool to be given the diminutive form. It is a holiday resort just across the river, linked to the city by a regular ferry service. Many Liverpudlians make frequent trips there. Other proper nouns affected are those denoting nationality or religion, though some of these are of much wider usage. Thus

Chinese are known as *Chinkies*, Americans as *Yankies*, and Protestants, when referred to by Catholics, become *Proddies*. The Salvation Army is usually called *The Sally Army*.

By far the largest group of nouns affected are count nouns, which fall into a number of main groups. One such group is that of occupations: *bricky* > *bricklayer*; *binny* > *bin-collector*; *docky-* > *docker*; *cusy* > *customs-officer*; *milky* > *milkman*; *parky* > *park-keeper*; *matchy* > *matchmaker* (these are employees of the match firm Bryant and May). Although the term for a 'gasmeter reader' is *gasy*, and 'electricity meter reader' is known as a *lecky man*. This is necessary to avoid confusion, as *lecky* is used for *electricity*. *Lecky*, however, was once used as a count noun. In the days when electric trams were common 'skipping leckies', which meant jumping on and off trams without paying, was a favourite game. Another homonym is *proey*. It can mean either a 'printed programme', usually for a football match, or a 'prostitute'. Presumably the context of the word makes its meaning clear.

One group of words classifies people by physical attributes, temperament or intelligence. Many of these, as would be expected, are back formations, the adjective being used as the base for the new noun formation; *baldy* 'bald-headed person'; *nudy* 'naked person'; *densy* 'stupid person'; *fatty* 'fat person'; *blacky* 'negro'; *skinny* 'thin person';. Another group of nouns describe the attributes themselves: *twiggies* 'thin legs'; *sidies* 'sideburns'; *bandies* 'bandy legs'; *mousy* 'moustache'.

Nouns for food form a fairly large group: *finny-haddy* > *Finnan haddock*; *roasty* > *roast potato*; *phally* 'banana' (from *phallic?*); *butty* 'slice of bread and butter' (especially in *chip-butty* and *jam-butty*); *bicky* 'biscuit' (this does not conform to the usual pattern, but is often found in the compound *chocky-bicky*); *(wet) nellies* 'Nelson cakes' (these are no longer sold in the shops and are referred to as one of the good things of the past. They were made from cake crumbs and broken biscuits soaked in syrup.)

Clothes are another group: *wooly* > *woollen jumper*; *suedies* > *suede shoes*; *cordies* > *corduroy trousers*; *pinny* > *pinafore*; *undies* > *underwear*; *cosy* or *swimmy* > *swimming costume*. Most of the above are fairly widespread through the country. The following miscellaneous terms, however, seem confined to Liverpool: *hosy* > *hospital*; *boozery (?)* 'brewery'; *bommy* > *bombsite*; *debby* 'bombsite' (from French *debris?*). In the same way *ally* > *Alsation dog* seems a fairly local usage, whereas *moggy* 'cat' is fairly widespread in the North. According to Partridge (1), *mog* is twentieth century schoolboy

128

slang for 'cat', and may come from the dialectal word *moggy* meaning 'animal'. The Liverpudlian usage may therefore be either the dialectal *moggy* used in a restricted sense, or the disyllabic form of *mog*.

A special area in which this diminutive is used by children is the game of marbles. The generic term is *ollies*, and this word is also used to marbles made of clay. More specialized terms are *glassies* for glass marbles, and *bolly* or *metally* for a ball-bearing used for the same purpose. Other children's words are *catty* for *catapult* and, taken from local boy scouts, *bivvy* for *bivouac* and *provvy* for *provisions*.

A final miscellany of count nouns is: *tranny* > *transistor*; *exy* > *X-film*; *lippy* > *lipstick*; *ciggy* > *cigarette*; *presy* > *present*. There is also the interesting *this afy* or *the safy* for 'this afternoon'. *Afy* is only used when preceded by *this*.

A few mass nouns have also been affected by this usage. Most of these are connected with food and drink: *chocky* > *chocolate*; *rolly* > *rolled bacon*; *conny onny* > *condensed milk*; *sterry* > *sterilized milk*; *bevvy* 'alcoholic drink' (probably from *beverage*). There is also *lecky* > *electricity*.

Examples of disyllabic abstract nouns are rare. I have found only two: *footy* > *football*; *hollies* > *holidays*. There are also two interesting cases where the part is used to denote the whole: *casey* 'football' (from *case*); and *shawlies* 'old women' (from the *shawls* they wear).

It is not only nouns which are affected, but also some verbs and adjectives. The dialectal verb forms, however, are rare, and all derive from nouns: *welly* 'to kick' (from *Wellington boot*; *toey* 'to kick with the toes' (as compared with the instep). The verb *golly* may have no connection with this usage. It means 'to spit', and is probably connected with the Australian slang term *golly* meaning 'spittoon'.

With adjectives it is difficult to decide whether the form derives from the diminutive -y or whether it is the -y commonly used in English as an adjectival ending. *plasy* > *plastic* and *lasy* > *elastic* are fairly clear uses of the diminutive. However *tatty* 'untidy', *narky* 'irritable' and *cobby* 'easily annoyed' probably derive respectively from *tat* 'a rag', *cob* as in *to have a cob on* meaning 'to be annoyed', and *nark* 'an irritable person'. If so, these three adjectives are formed by means of the common adjectival suffix. *Narky*, however, may be borrowed from Australian, in which case the noun *nark* may be a backformation. There is a similar difficulty with *eggy* 'irritated', from the verb *egg*, meaning 'tease'. *Plainy* 'plain' is found only in a rhyme used in a children's ball game.

Other adjectives in *-y* which are used in Liverpool and elsewhere are *mardy* 'whining', *mingy* 'mean' and *diddy* 'small'. *Banny* 'broken' is only found in the expression *banny-mug*, used of the broken crockery children play with. I have, however, found two examples of adjectives which seem to be the disyllabic form of other adjectives. *Grotty* 'new or new-fangled but useless' probably derives from *grotesque*. According to Partridge the word was popularized by the Beatles and was commonly used among young people from 1962. *Possy* is derived from *positive*, with the same meaning. Thus 'I'm possy' means 'I'm sure'.

Much of the above was discussed with the student during tutorials. It is interesting how her attitude towards her material changed during this period. When it was suggested that she examine this more limited set of data rather than her more extensive collection of 'quaint' expressions, her first reaction was 'How can disyllables be interesting? Ridiculous!' It is not difficult to infer from her handling of the text, however, that she did become engrossed in it.

What exactly were the roles played by tutor and student during these meetings it is impossible to define precisely. On the whole the initiative was left with the student, the tutor being concerned primarily to discuss the advantages and disadvantages of the student's suggestions and to offer suitable terms where necessary. The actual arrangement of the material and handling of the terms were left entirely to the student.

This seems to have worked quite well, and there is only one major area where the tutor might perhaps have exerted more influence. This is in connection with the ordering of the sections. As we have it, the student places her treatment of the changes in pronunciation brought about by the diminutive after the section which we have just quoted. A more careful examination of the implications of this ordering would have placed it in front of this section. This would have had the effect of easing the difficulties of the student considerably in the description of her text. The best way to explain what we mean is by example.

At the end of the passage just quoted the student writes *possy* for the derived form of *positive*. The problem is how to establish a consistent spelling in non-standard forms without ambiguity as to the pronunciation (and without having to go too deeply into problems of phonetic transcription). The spelling we have gives the impression to the reader that *possy* rhymes with *bossy*, which is not the case. At the same time, if the word were spelled *posy*, we should have a pronunciation rhyming with *rosy*. This would give the correct value for the medial consonant, but the wrong value for the first vowel. To be consistent with both standard English spelling patterns and accuracy, the spelling *pozzy* would seem to answer the case. But this seems too far from the original *positive* to indicate the link between the two, which is perhaps why the student did not think of it.

The point we are making is that, if the phonological section had preceded the morphological section instead of the other way about, such problems would have emerged and could have been fairly easily resolved. The solution would have been either to use a phonetic transcription throughout or, preferably, to establish a consistent convention of spelling for the derived forms. This latter would have satisfied both the demands of accuracy and the student's desire to weigh the morphological treatment more heavily than the phonological.

The purpose of making this point here is to show how important it is for the tutor to try and be aware of difficulties that might not emerge except over a period of time. In this particular case the point did not come out until after the student had completed the project, when it was too late; so that the tutor failed the student in an area where just a little forethought could have eased her path considerably.

Another consequence of this suggested reordering of the material might have been to avoid another weakness of this study, which is that the section in which the sound changes brought about by the addition of this diminutive is too brief. This illustrates well a constraint mentioned earlier in Chapter 3 when we suggested caution in allowing a student to become too enthusiastic about dialect studies. One of the drawbacks of our method of approaching language study is that, except under optimum conditions, teachers do not have enough time to spend with students in order to explore with sufficient delicacy the descriptive issues raised by phonetics. It is therefore easy, as we feel happened in this case, for the teacher to play down phonology, and this has the effect of the student not giving it the attention it deserves.

Her section on the sound changes that occur with this diminutive is quite good in terms of the sources available to her:

131

Words with the -*y* diminutive can also be classified according to the sound preceding the suffix. All the examples in this study can be classed according to whether the -*y* is preceded by a vowel or consonant, and each of these groups further classified according to the way each sound is articulated ((3) pp 24 and 26).

In the consonant group the -*y* is often preceded by a fricative. When the fricative is [f] or [θ], it becomes voiced [v], [ð] before -y, e.g. *sevy* [sɛvi] *Sefton Park; avy* [avi] *afternoon; smithy* [smiði] *Smith*. In the case of [s], however, this seems to happen only after short vowels. Thus we can compare *gasy* [gazi], 'gas-meter collector'; *lesy* [lɛzi] 'Lesbian'; *hosy* [hɔzi] 'hospital' with *casey* [ka:si] 'football'; *vauxy* [vɔ:ksi] 'Vauxhall Road'; *leecey* [li:si] 'Leece Street'.

Notice, however, that *mousy* 'moustache' is pronounced with the voice [z]; and that the [s] of *densy* 'dense' remains unvoiced (this is one of the few places where the suffix is preceded by a consonant cluster.).

The fricative [ʃ] remains unvoiced at all times, thus: *tishy* 'tissue'; *marshy* 'Marsh Lane Street'; *squashy* 'squashed chocolate'. All other consonants remain unchanged. (There are no examples of which I know in which the sound [ŋ] preceded the -*y*.)

There are very few examples of words in which the suffix is used immediately after a vowel. The only cases I know are where a certain amount of lip-rounding is found before the -*y*; *cowy* 'Co-op'; *newy* 'New Brighton'; *mowy* 'mouth'.

Despite its shortcomings, the student found a certain impetus from looking at this aspect of the work that she later found useful. At the very least, she has not been as reluctant to use and read unfamiliar symbols as she would otherwise have been.

Her final section is short. She merely relates the text briefly to the wider context and looks to the future:

The number of words on which this essay is based is not very large, but I think it is a fair sample because the collection is drawn from a wide range of people and most of the words I have heard many times. Also, the number of words in the dialect affected by this trend is limited. Not all well-known places, for example, become disyllabic, because the Liverpudlian has other sources to draw upon to bring about variety. One such, his love of humour and metaphor, is capable of producing quite a variety of expressions. For example, Liverpool's Roman Catholic Cathedral is known variously as *Paddy's Wigwam*, *The Mersey Funnel* and *The Birthday Cake*.

Words affected by the trend are commonly used words which belong to a few main categories. These become disyllabic according to the rules I have outlined. It seems unlikely that the rules will change. For example, they fit in well with the text of Spiegl's books, which are now over six years old. Present change merely indicates that more words are formed within the rules as old ones die.

Bibliography and References
(1) Partridge, E. *A Dictionary of Slang and Unconventional English*, vols 1 and 2. R.K.P. London, 1967.
(2) Spiegl, F. *Lern Yerself Scouse* Scouse Press, Liverpool, 1966
(3) Jones, D. *The Pronunciation of English* C.U.P., 1958; Spiegl, F. *The ABZ of Scouse* Scouse Press, Liverpool, 1966.

We are grateful to the student for allowing us to quote her study in full. If we have been critical of various aspects of it, this is intended in no sense to be critical of the student herself, but rather of ourselves in that we were unable at that time to offer the kind of help which a longer experience in doing this kind of work has brought more within our capabilities. What does impress us about the work is that it achieved the quality it did, considering the tutor's lack of experience within the area. We feel it goes a long way to justify our claim that students have a great potential for studying language, if only they are offered the opportunity to realize it.

We recently asked this student, some three years after she completed the project, what she felt she had gained from doing this particular topic. A summary of her reply is interesting.

In the first place, she felt that having been put in a position to discover and utilize a few technical terms relating to language was useful. This was not only because they had some use in themselves, but also because it constrained her to see the desirability for being explicit. To put it another way, for the first time she was compelled to think about the need for a level of descriptive adequacy; and was able to generalize about this from language to other fields.

Secondly, since three quarters of the work involved classifying and sorting, she became involved for the first time in work which was quite different from the work she had previously associated with 'English'—that is, either a personal 'response' or the kind of critical approach associated with A-levels. And since this language work involved a considerable degree of asking questions derived from hypotheses, she began to learn something about the nature of 'research' in an original way.

Thirdly, she felt that the research she was undertaking was into an area that was largely unexplored. As she herself put it, because the area of investigation was narrow, she believed that she had well exploited it and found that to do so was very satisfying. 'Nobody else had done this.'

Fourthly, she had discovered that first impressions in language are not always the best. She had become quite taken with the idea that 'so much could come out of so little'. Another way of putting this, of course, is to say that it is not the language which is interesting, but rather the way in which the language is approached.

Fifthly, in having to write up her study, she found that a literary essay was not the only kind of structure that was viable. She described how, to a large extent, the study wrote itself once she had sorted out her material to her own satisfaction. It is remarkable how many students find it difficult to accept that 'proper essays' can even be allowed to have sub-titles. If we may generalize on this, it would seem that this student now discovered for the first time, at least in practice, the notion that there are varieties of language within the written mode, even within the category 'essay.' Personally, we find it disturbing that the system through which she had been did not allow this to happen sooner.

In conclusion, we might only say that we hope these simple projects, along with our comments and suggestions, will provide the impetus for other teachers and lecturers, with some confidence, to guide their students to explore some aspects of 'real' language and to produce similar or better language projects. We realise only too well that there are few ideal students and even fewer ideal situations, and we hope, with a little ingenuity, that our suggested procedure is flexible enough to be adapted to both large classes and inflexible timetables. And so we end where we began, with the comments of the same student who recorded the dialogue with which we began our first chapter, between the gardener and the lecturer. As this book has been essentially about the work of students, it seems appropriate to give one of them the last word:

I started off this project in a light-hearted spirit, expecting to be amused and produce an entertaining contrast between two entirely different speakers, one with a strong local dialect and of limited education and the other a university lecturer and presumably a speaker of standard English with a prestige accent.... I got a laugh but it was not the one I expected. It was only when

134

I got the words written down on paper that I realised there was more in both the language and the situation than I thought. What I learnt from the study was how easy it is to make superficial judgments on people like George from the way they speak. If it is true that 'manners Makyth the man', how much more true it is that language reveals the man who speaks it but that we as observers can only overcome these superficial judgments by a much closer scrutiny of what a man says and how he says it.

Notes

1.

As introductory volumes to some of the aspects of language taken up in this book, we recommend the Penguin series, including J. D. O'Connor's *Phonetics*, Frank Palmer's *Grammar*, Leech's *Semantics*, and David Crystal's *Linguistics*.

2.

[1] A discussion of phatic communion and its social significance can be found in Ogden and Richard's *The Meaning of Meaning* (Routledge and Kegan Paul). Chapters 4 and 5 in Crystal and Davy's *Investigating English Style* (Longman) deal with 'Conversation' and 'Unscripted Commentary' respectively. Detailed and sociologically-oriented work on conversational analysis of a sophisticated nature is associated with, among others, the names of H. Sacks and E. Schegloff. A selection of their work can be found in D. Sudnow (ed.), *Studies in Social Interaction*, Free Press, 1972.

[2] 'Meaning potential' is difficult to define briefly. In Halliday's words, 'The potential of language is a meaning potential. This meaning potential is the linguistic realization of the behaviour potential; "can mean" is "can do" when translated into language. The meaning potential is in turn realized in the language system as lexico-grammatical potential, which is what the speaker "can say".'

[3] A number of linguists have been concerned with describing the functions of language. Halliday proposes what he calls certain 'macro-functions' as the 'abstract representations of the basic functions which language is made to serve'. These 'macro-functions' include the 'ideational', the 'interpersonal' and the 'textual' functions of language. M. A. K. Halliday, *Explorations in the Functions of Language*, (Edward Arnold, 1973) Chapter 2. James Britton classifies the functions of language differently; he divides them into the 'transactional', which is subdivided into the 'conative' and the 'informative', the 'expressive' and the 'poetic'. James Britton, *Language and Learning*, (Pelican, 1970).

136

3.

[1] Discussions of dialect and register are too numerous for mention of more than a few. The book most relevant to the school situation is Peter Trudgill's *Accent, Dialect and the School*, in this series, which is a comprehensive and thoughtful treatment. Alan Davies in 'The Notion of Register' and Andrew Philp in 'Informal Study of Register' (*The Educational Review*, 'The State of Language', Vol. 22, No. 1) are also concerned with the classroom, as are Doughty, Pearce and Thornton in *Exploring Language* (Edward Arnold). Geoffrey Turner includes a useful chapter on register in his book on *Stylistics* (Penguin) and useful general discussions are to be found in Halliday, McIntosh and Strevens *The Linguistic Sciences and Language Teaching* (Longman), Peter Strevens *Papers in Language and Language Teaching* (O.U.P.), Randolph Quirk *The Use of English* (Longman). For a sophisticated and sociologically-oriented approach, see Ruqaiya Hasan's chapter in Basil Bernstein's *Class, Codes and Control*, Vol. II (Routledge and Kegan Paul). Gerald Brook in his book *Varieties of English* (Macmillan) includes separate chapters on register, dialect and idiolect, and Martin Wakelin has written in greater detail on dialects in *English Dialects* (Athlone).

[2] According to Labov, there is some doubt whether 'bidialectal' speakers actually exist. For a discussion of this point, see W. Labov, *Sociolinguistic Patterns* (University of Pennsylvania Press, 1972), pp. 215–16.

[3] W. Labov, *The Social Stratification of English in New York City*, Washington D.C.: Center for Applied Linguistics, 1966. P. Trudgill, *The Social Differentiation of English in Norwich*, Cambridge U.P. (1974).

4.

[1] Probably for the non-specialist the most useful books of the many which have been written in the area are D. Barnes, J. Britton, H. Rosen, *Language, the Learner and the School*, (Penguin, 1969), D. Barnes, *From Communication to Curriculum* (Penguin, 1975), J. McH. Sinclair and R. M. Coulthard, *Towards an Analysis of Discourse* (O.U.P. 1975) and M. Coulthard, *An Introduction to Discourse Analysis* (Longman, 1977).

[2] The concept of 'illocutionary force' was first discussed by linguistic philosophers and further explored in an article by J. Boyd and J. P. Thorne, 'The Semantics of Modal Verbs', *Journal of Linguistics*, Vol. 5 (1969) pp. 57–74. Of more relevance to the classroom is the discussion in Sinclair and Coulthard's *Towards an Analysis of Discourse*, mentioned above and, Coulthard's *An Introduction to Discourse Analysis*, Chaps. 3 and 5.

5.

For examples of detailed descriptions of written texts, see Crystal and Davy, *Investigating English Style* (Longman) and Geoffrey Leech, *English in Advertising* (Longman). For a less explicitly linguistic approach, see John Pearce 'Diversity in Written English', *Exploring Language* (Edward Arnold, 1972).

Appendix

Selected List of Titles of Projects already undertaken

A Derbyshire great uncle
A Nottingham landlady
An Australian visitor
*Written language of a young
    brother 5–7*
The humour of Spike Milligan
A nurse talking about her job
The language of young twins
*Children's storytelling in
    response to pictures*
Jamaican schoolchildren
*London and Lancashire
    grandparents*
*Discussion in a Geography
    lesson*
How adults talk to children
Table talk in the family
*A group of students living
    together*
A committee at work
A group of hippies
Auctioneers
Market stallholders
Art critics
Disc jockies
Estate agents
Travel brochures
*Radio and TV sports
    commentaries*
News *bulletins on Radios
    1, 2, 3 and 4*

Sermons of different priests
Levels of formality in school
*How different newspapers
    report the same news*
Children's TV programmes
*Newspaper advertising:
    1770, 1870, 1970*
Perfume advertisements
Hotel menus
*Do some newspapers use longer
    words than others?*
Interjections in comics
Class bias in strip cartoons
Language of teenage comics
Humour in advertising
Sunday supplement advertisements
Woman's Own Problem Page
Greetings cards
Postcards
Language of death
Factory notices
Business letters from abroad
Football songs
*How a folk song changes in
    time*
Children's slang
Legal language
The language of elocution
The language of guidebooks
The changing story of Tom Thumb
The speeches of Churchill

138

The Merchant of Venice:	*American football*
Shakespeare and Lamb	*Franglais*
A Yorkshire dialect play	*How fast do we speak?*
A Victorian Children's Book	*Pausing in speech*

During the past five years we have supervised more than 400 Language Projects. Many of these were duplicates in some way or another. For example, comparing newspapers with one another has proved to be a very popular choice. The above list of abbreviated titles is meant to show the range of topics possible for this kind of work and to serve as a possible starting point for expansion. We have not tried to group the titles into areas, since we feel this to be an impossibility. Nevertheless we have tried to put topics which have a similar feel about them next to each other as far as possible.

139